PARTICIPATORY RESEARCH

Working with vulnerable groups in research and practice

Jo Aldridge

D1615277

First published in Great Britain in 2016 by

Policy Press
University of Bristol
1-9 Old Park Hill
Bristol BS2 8BB
UK
t: +44 (0)117 954 5940
tpp-info@bristol.ac.uk
www.policypress.co.uk

North America office:
Policy Press
c/o The University of Chicago Press
1427 East 60th Street
Chicago, IL 60637, USA
t: +1 773 702 7700
f: +1 773-702-9756
sales@press.uchicago.edu
www.press.uchicago.edu

© Policy Press 2016

British Library Cataloguing in Publication Data
A catalogue record for this book is available from the British Library

Library of Congress Cataloging-in-Publication Data
A catalog record for this book has been requested

ISBN 978-1-4473-2555-0 paperback
ISBN 978-1-4473-2556-7 ePub
ISBN 978-1-4473-2557-4 Mobi

Cover design by Policy Press
Front cover image: istock
Printed and bound in Great Britain by CPI Group (UK) Ltd, Croydon, CR0 4YY
Policy Press uses environmentally responsible print partners

To my sons, Jack and Luke.

With love, always.

Contents

About the author

Jo Aldridge is Professor of Social Policy and Criminology in the Department of Social Sciences, Loughborough University, UK. She also directs the Young Carers Research Group, which is known both nationally and internationally for its pioneering work with children and young people who have caring responsibilities in the home. In her research she works mainly with vulnerable children and young people, people with learning difficulties and mental health problems and women victims-survivors of domestic violence. She specialises in participatory research methods and research ethics.

Acknowledgements

This book would not have been possible without the valuable contributions of the numerous research participants I have had the pleasure and privilege to work with over a number of years. Without the patience, energy and commitment of those people whose lives and experiences are often challenging and painful, and who took part in the research projects described in the chapters of this book, we would not have the insight and understanding we now have with respect to the experiences and needs of young carers, people with learning difficulties and women victims–survivors of domestic violence. My extended thanks and gratitude go to all of these people. Grateful acknowledgement also goes to the funders of the research projects described in Chapters Two, Three and Four, specifically Rethink, the Economic and Social Research Council (ESRC) and the Big Lottery Fund. Many thanks also to Alison Shaw, Laura Vickers, Laura Greaves and others at Policy Press for their patience, help and support throughout the writing and publication process, and also to the reviewer who made such helpful comments on the first draft of the book.

Introduction

In the last 40 years or so there has been a notable shift towards greater collaboration in research (and practice), and specifically in participatory research (PR), which has provided new opportunities for equalising, and even transposing, researcher–participant relationships and facilitating participant 'voice'. As disciplinary boundaries have become more fluid, this change has been important in enabling researchers to work more effectively with participants in research who may be considered vulnerable, marginalised or socially excluded. However, despite this change, not all research that claims to work more collaboratively or inclusively with participants demonstrates clearly and rigorously how this is achieved and with reference to specific and clearly defined participatory methods and models. This book aims to address these issues, concepts and oversights by exploring in closer detail the interconnections between research methodology and praxis, and specifically PR that aims to facilitate and advance inclusive or 'emancipatory' methods and approaches with vulnerable or marginalised groups.

The association between vulnerability and participation is an important one, not least because people who may be defined as vulnerable or marginalised – whether innately, uniquely or circumstantially (see the discussion in Chapter One) – are often overlooked or denied full participation in research, either because they are considered 'hard to reach' or access in order to recruit successfully on to studies, or because the ethical considerations and procedures involved in doing so are seen as problematic, challenging, or even insurmountable. The result is that certain vulnerable or marginalised individuals or groups (specifically, for example, those who may be defined as multiply vulnerable) may be left out of studies altogether, and thus our knowledge and insights about their experiences and needs remains limited. However, 'vulnerability' is both a contested and mutable concept that is often determined by context and the perspective of those who are 'doing the defining', so to speak. Thus, both empirically, as well as with respect to contemporary health and social care discourses, vulnerability is an issue that needs to be addressed conceptually, philosophically and in practical terms (including ethically) – these issues are explored further in Chapter One.

Underpinning or connecting the twin concepts of vulnerability and participation in the book is the notion of narrative – epistemologically, and as research method and analytical technique – which is explored in detail in Chapter One, and which is also relevant to the specific PR examples described and discussed in each of the chapters that follow in this book. One of the prominent features and, indeed, advantages of narrative research is its broad, all embracing, inter-disciplinary nature where life history, autobiographical and storytelling approaches are used across a range of disciplines. In many respects, these broader definitions of narrative research allow for more catholic and diverse interpretations of narrative techniques within the qualitative field more generally, and can therefore facilitate a degree of methodological innovation and creativity (see Chapter One). Narrative research also provides researchers with opportunities for working with small numbers of participants using intensive, individualised or subjective methods that are often necessary when working more inclusively with vulnerable or marginalised individuals or groups. Research that adopts these kinds of approaches is explored in detail in the book by drawing on evidence from a wide range of narrative and participatory studies. However, the book's main focus is on specific vulnerable populations and examples of PR that demonstrate different ways of working with marginalised (or socially excluded) participants using methods that enhance participant 'voice'.

Thus, each of the chapters considers PR from the perspective of different vulnerable groups, for example, children and young people (with a specific focus on research on young carers and their families; see Chapter Two); people with learning difficulties (Chapter Three); and victims of abuse and trauma (specifically, women victims-survivors of domestic violence; see Chapter Four). The focus on these different participant groups not only reflects my own interest in and research with these groups over a number of years, but also demonstrates the importance of recognising and addressing the needs of participants in PR who are multiply vulnerable or marginalised. Thus, each chapter and, indeed, the book as a whole, also represents to some extent a personal reflexive journey through participatory methods, even though the elements of participation in the projects discussed – as measured against the Participatory Model described and discussed in Chapter Six, for example (see Figure 6.1) – may vary considerably.

The intention of the book, however, is not to be reflexive simply for the sake of it, or to privilege the perspective and 'expertise' of the 'professional' researcher (see the discussion in Chapter Five), but to contribute new knowledge and insights about different participatory methods and techniques, as well as practical issues such as ethical regulations and procedures, for example, that can help prioritise the perspectives and 'voices' of participants themselves. In 'emancipatory' terms, this is evidenced particularly through the examples of participatory visual and autobiographical narrative methods described in Chapters Two, Three and Four. Such methods are essential in effective PR and especially when working with multiply vulnerable or marginalised individuals or groups who, in certain instances, apart from being more difficult to identify, access and recruit on to studies, may also be unwilling or unable to participate in research studies that use conventional methods. This may be true even in qualitative research where (conventional) methods such as interviewing or focus groups are used that rely on a degree of abstract reasoning, memory performance and verbal contribution from the participants involved. For many people, this simply isn't feasible. Thus, more flexible and personalised, even 'bespoke', methods are needed that incorporate different approaches, and specifically narrative techniques, that can facilitate alternative interpretations and manifestations of participation and 'voice'.

The examples of PR studies referred to and described in each of the chapters demonstrate, in different ways, the kinds of research methods that emphasise these alternative approaches to participation, and particularly techniques that require different sensory skills and contributions from participants. This is demonstrated in research projects with very young children and children whose lives and experiences are both challenging and painful (for example, young carers; see Chapter Two), as well as in research with people with profound learning difficulties (Chapter Three). Both of these participant groups require methods in PR that rely on different sensory contributions, such as visual methods, including participatory visual and elicitation techniques. Women victims-survivors of domestic violence not only require methods of participation that aim to minimise risk and harm, but also that serve to counteract their experiences of abuse and violence that are so often distinguished by powerlessness and lack of control and agency in intimate relationships. As such, methods that enhance women's personal autonomy, control and emancipation are essential, and especially those that engender a personal sense of 'being believed'. The participatory narrative research (PNR) project described in Chapter Four demonstrates these aspects of PR, which are further enhanced by the inclusion of Rosie's account of domestic violence in the second half of the chapter. Rosie's account is presented in full and unedited (alongside some of her personal reflections on her narrative in Chapter Five), as part of the multi-phase approach adopted in the PNR project.

While this book is aimed primarily at researchers, academics and students of social policy, health and social care, and related fields, it should also be of interest to practitioners in health and social care who work with vulnerable, marginalised or socially excluded people (as, for example, service users and patients). Indeed, there has been a notable shift in professional practice in recent years across a range of disciplines that demonstrate the synergies between research and practice, and particularly with respect to participatory or more inclusive approaches. Thus, we have seen the development of new social work, health and therapeutic practices with vulnerable service users using less conventional approaches, such as narrative and creative writing techniques, as well as reflexivity as a pedagogic tool to help professionals understand and develop their working practices (these developments are discussed further in Chapter Five).

In each of the chapters it is recognised that any effective participatory project must also adopt and adhere to appropriate ethical procedures that are rigorous and consistent, and which are often distinguished by both instrumental and more intuitive approaches that ensure ethical participation is also part of an ongoing process of consultation throughout the course of any project. The challenge for the researcher (and practitioner) planning to work with vulnerable or marginalised people in more inclusive ways, however, is to adopt approaches that recognise their competency and agency – aligned conceptually and epistemologically to contemporary shifts in understanding about rights and needs – while at the same time that work within research governance and ethical frameworks and classifications that define them as vulnerable.

In order for researchers to address these challenges effectively, greater clarity, rigour and consistency are called for in PR that demonstrate the validity and rigour of participatory methods and that can, for example, also give clear directions for policy and practice. Despite Thomas and O'Kane's claim in the late 1990s that PR has the potential to 'assist with reliability and validity' (1998, p 336), how this can be achieved with reference to recognised models, typologies or frames of reference is something that, to date, has been largely missing from the PR literature. This issue is discussed in more detail in Chapter Six and with reference to the Participatory Model (Figure 6.1) that incorporates different levels, or domains, of participation. The model was developed with the primary intention of presenting researchers (and professionals) with a useful device for planning and assessing past, current or future PR projects in terms of the extent and limitations of their participatory objectives.

What is important in considering and promoting more inclusive, participatory approaches in PR, and particularly among marginalised or vulnerable groups (and what can further help in terms of lending greater validity and rigour to PR methods), is the need to move away from research that treats participants as objects of study towards a more emancipatory approach that not only facilitates greater collaboration and equality in research relationships, but also research methods that promote self-advocacy and transposition of research roles. The different domains included and described in the Participatory Model described in Chapter Six illustrate how these objectives can be achieved in participatory approaches that allow for a degree of fluidity and movement across domains, but which must always advance away from research that is tokenistic and treats participants simply as objects of study (see Figure 6.1). As discussed further in Chapter Six, where research involves working with vulnerable or marginalised participants, the intention should be, as far as possible, to adopt participatory methods that involve participants as social actors and even as self-advocates, even though, as Christensen and Prout (2002, p 482) observe, this may, 'be seen as unsettling previous unquestioned research practices and understandings.'

A further challenge for researchers (and practitioners) who work with vulnerable groups using participatory methods – and particularly for those who work with inevitably small numbers of marginalised or socially excluded people – is how to transform personal meaning-making into something more meaningful in broader social, political and cultural contexts. As Walmsley and Johnson (2003, p 31) have argued, there is a responsibility 'on the part of the researcher and participants to ensure that [research] is used to positive effect in the society or the organization in which it is undertaken.' For many researchers, one of the main reasons for choosing to adopt participatory approaches is the opportunity they present to give participants a voice in research as well as in public and political discourses, and to build on relationships based on understanding and mutuality. However, achieving participatory and personal and social change objectives in PR is not always a straightforward process, and there may be a degree of tension or conflict at the point at which these concepts and principles intersect.

In many respects, one of the fundamental aims of this book is to demonstrate the importance, as well as some of the challenges, in PR when working with vulnerable or marginalised individuals or groups, and the ways in which these challenges and tensions may be addressed and overcome. A number of strategies for meeting these challenges are highlighted throughout the book but are also brought together in a set of participatory principles that recognise the need for greater clarity and rigour in PR design (and that complement the Participatory Model domains; see Chapter Six). Importantly, these strategies and principles allow for and, indeed, promote a degree of methodological flexibility and creativity in PR that help advance more genuine and meaningful participation in research for those who take part.

ONE

Participation, 'vulnerability' and voice

Emergence of participatory research

Engaging research respondents in participatory research (PR) methods that promote the autonomy and 'voices' of people defined as vulnerable has gained prominence over recent years. From the 1970s, new developments and approaches in qualitative methodologies in the health and social sciences allowed for, and indeed embraced, more creative methods of investigation in a post-modern, post-structuralist era. The result was that new and more diverse empirical approaches began to flourish across a range of different disciplines, and significantly, to address issues of vulnerability, inclusion and participation, although the connection or parity between these concepts were not always made explicit in research design and discourses. This chapter considers the emergence of PR, including participatory action research (PAR), in the context of these new and developing research methodologies in the social sciences, and in other disciplines and fields, and also explores and contextualises the concept of vulnerability and its relationship with, and relevance to, PR methods and techniques. Particular emphasis is on the role of PR in facilitating and promoting engagement with vulnerable or marginalised individuals and groups in more direct and inclusive ways.

In their 1995 review of PR, Cornwall and Jewkes asked the fundamental question, 'if all research involves participation, what makes research participatory?' (p 1668), and this question remains a pertinent one even today, warranting closer examination. Although the terms 'participatory research' and 'participatory action research' are often conflated or are used interchangeably at times, the former is a somewhat broad umbrella under which a number of participatory, collaborative or inclusive research methods and approaches are located. PAR, on the other hand, which emerged in the 1940s following the pioneering work of Kurt Lewin and the Tavistock Institute (see Chevalier and Buckles, 2013), emphasises specifically social change outcomes for groups, organisations or communities through *action* research. As Chevalier and Buckles argue (2013, p 4), developments

7

in PAR mean that it 'now represents a well documented tradition of active-risk taking and experimentation in social reflectivity backed up by evidential reasoning and learning through experience and real action.' PAR also involves a diversity of approaches or techniques including participatory rural appraisal (PRA), participatory learning and action (PLA), as well as participatory visual methods and so on.

Chataway's (1997) study with Native communities of North America is a good example of the PAR approach, which embraced collaboration and mutuality. Chataway's research focused on issues of identity, security and self-government using and modifying the PAR approach through the use of focus groups and intergroup discussions, and enabling community participants to draw on 'non-Native' research strategies to identify reasons for community divisions and the barriers to change. Given the level of political oppression the Native population had experienced under 'Euro-American dominance', and the subsequent distrust of 'outsiders' within communities, the researchers were required to be flexible and adaptable with respect to PAR approaches and methods. They understood that the study needed to be both 'internally directed' as well as in the best interests of the participants if it was to be successful. Chataway concluded that without a PAR approach, 'we would not have been able to overcome the barriers to research in this context. With PAR, we were able to complete four successive pieces of *collaborative* research' (p 748; emphasis added; for a full discussion about different kinds of PAR approaches, see Chevalier and Buckles, 2013).

The intention of PR more broadly (conceptually and philosophically, for example) is to promote inclusion and collaboration and to recognise and give credence to the voices of both individuals and communities in social research (see Fals Borda, 1988; Whyte, 1989; McTaggart, 1997; Goodley and Moore, 2000; O'Neill et al, 2002; Aldridge, 2007, 2012a, 2012b). Furthermore, both PR and PAR draw on philosophical principles and ideas that relate to mutuality and understanding in research practices, and are 'designed to promote active involvement' in the research process by those who, in other more conventional methods, may be treated simply as the objects of research (Chataway, 1997, p 747; see also Fals Borda, 1988; Whyte, 1989; Reason, 1993; Bourdieu, 1996; McTaggart, 1997). Writing in the 1970s, Rapoport (1970, p 499) proposed that PR differed from other types of qualitative research in the immediacy of researchers' active involvement in research processes, with a specific focus on 'joint collaboration with a mutually acceptable ethical framework.'

Thus, while the types of methods used in PR (and PAR) studies can be diverse and embrace techniques adopted and adapted from other disciplines and practices, the fundamental difference between PR and other research methodologies lies in 'the location of power in the various stages of the research process' (Cornwall and Jewkes, 1995, p 1667), and the fact that, in the main, the stories and 'voices' of participants are placed centre stage, both in the design and objectives of participatory approaches. Walmsley and Johnson (2003, p 10) recognise this methodological diversity in PR studies that have been described variously as 'participatory, action or emancipatory (Freire, 1970, Reason, 1994)', but that all have a common objective and intention to engage more effectively with participants and in ways that facilitate more empathic and democratising approaches to research participation. The authors describe this type of approach, as well as their own PR with people with learning difficulties, as 'inclusive' research, where participants 'are active participants, not only as subjects but also as initiators, doers, writers and disseminators of research' (p 9; see also Chapter Three; and Atkinson, 1986; Flynn, 1989; Jahoda et al, 1989).

Interestingly, debates in disability research, as well as in the field of learning difficulty research (see Chappell, 2000; Chappell et al, 2001), emphasise the distinction between PR and emancipatory research where the latter is distinguished by its alliance with the social model of disability, and where all stages of the research process are controlled by people with disabilities themselves (for a full discussion, see Chapter Three).

More generally, O'Neill and colleagues (2002, p 69) argue that participatory methods have helped to 'transgress conventional or traditional ways of analysing and representing research data' at a time when ideas about 'hard-to-reach' or marginalised groups in research were also changing – developing discourses in health and social care that had previously referred to and included 'disadvantaged' individuals were also being replaced by those that recognised and described the impact of social exclusion on 'vulnerable' individuals, groups and communities.

Despite these advances in methods terms and the opportunities offered by PR, critical questions remained (and remain) about the nature and extent of participation in these new types of approaches and their relevance to research with vulnerable or marginalised populations. Further debate or dialogue is also needed with respect to approaches that promote collaboration based on joint participant–researcher interaction and others that favour or embrace 'emancipatory' research, which allows for, and indeed promotes, role transformation in research (see Oliver, 1997; and for a full discussion, see Chapters Three and Five). While participatory methods and projects have developed and advanced over the past four decades, the advantages of using participatory techniques in research with vulnerable or marginalised individuals or groups also warrant closer examination and further exploration.

Undoubtedly, while the shift to more creative, less conventional research methods in recent years has helped those working with vulnerable people in social (and health) research develop and advance participatory methods, it is clear that not all research with vulnerable or marginalised groups embraces and promotes a participatory agenda or aligns itself specifically with PR or PAR objectives (nor are participatory methods only used among vulnerable respondents). Furthermore, not all research projects that lay claim to an inclusive, participatory agenda necessarily promote the principles associated with participatory approaches – such as understanding, mutuality, emancipation, collaboration, giving 'voice' and so on. Thus, when considering the opportunities offered by PR to address and embrace these concepts and ideals appropriately and effectively when working with vulnerable or marginalised participants, it is necessary from the outset to understand what is meant by vulnerability according to different perspectives and contexts. It is also important to explore and understand the relevance of participatory projects to researching so-called vulnerable populations and the ways in which individual and collective 'voices' are facilitated and heard in research praxis. Finally, it is necessary to identify and consider different models or typologies of participation in research that can help lend clarity, cohesion and rigour to PR in broader contexts, and demonstrate its worth as a valuable and 'valid' methodological tool.

Concepts of vulnerability in research, policy and practice

The intention of this book, and the examples of PR projects described in each chapter that promote PR methods, is to make clearer the link between participatory approaches and techniques and the opportunities they present in terms of working more collaboratively and empathically in research with vulnerable/marginalised individuals, specifically, those who are excluded from society or who are not necessarily connected to, or part of, a recognised organisation, locality or community, and who might otherwise be overlooked in research studies that use conventional approaches (because the nature of their vulnerability or marginalisation may make them hard to reach and recruit onto studies using conventional methods). Undoubtedly, less conventional participative qualitative methods lend themselves more readily to the flexibility and adaptability of approaches necessary when working with vulnerable/marginalised participants, including children and young people, people with learning difficulties and mental health problems, and victims of abuse or trauma (see Chapters Two, Three and Four; see also Etherington, 2000; Pritchard and Sainsbury, 2004; Aldridge, 2007, 2012a, 2012b; Bolton et al, 2011).

However, in many respects, vulnerability remains a mutable and even contestable concept. This is especially the case when considering the various definitions and classifications adopted in research governance and ethical frameworks, in health and social care discourses, and with respect to the self-perceptions of those people defined as 'vulnerable'. It is also clear that in many instances, research projects that lay claim to work inclusively with vulnerable populations (and even those that don't) do not always define vulnerability with specific reference to the project at hand, nor is it necessarily discussed in sufficient detail in order to demonstrate clearly the connection between research objectives, methods and practice.

Larkin (2009) acknowledges the universal relevance and use of the term 'vulnerable' both conceptually and in practice, but also recognises that the range of different interpretations of vulnerability (for different individuals and groups) renders a precise definition 'elusive'. She also proposes that 'its meaning also varies according to the context in which it is used' (p 1). In health and social care discourses it is most often used to denote susceptibility to harm or risk, for example, or as an indicator of enhanced need. Larkin, for example, cites the Department of Health definition of vulnerability (2000, Section 2.3), in which the lack of capacity for self-care determines a person's vulnerable status. She also refers to legislation, specifically, the Safeguarding Vulnerable Groups Bill (2006), in which a vulnerable person is someone who is in receipt of health or social care services, is living in sheltered accommodation, in prison or on probation, or someone who 'requires assistance in the conduct of their affairs' (Larkin, 2009, p 3). In her own research, Larkin herself makes distinctions between someone who is individually, uniquely and innately vulnerable themselves or who is vulnerable because of their circumstances, environment or as a result of structural factors or influences. The overlapping nature of vulnerability with victimisation and other forms of troubled–troublesome categorisations is also seen as particularly problematic.

While it would seem, then, that both conceptually and specifically anyone has the potential to be vulnerable at any given time according to different types of classifications, individuals are often grouped together under general categories of vulnerability. Rogers (1997), for example, identifies vulnerable groups as the very young and the very old, those susceptible to illness, black and minority ethnic (BME) groups, people on low income or who are unemployed, as well as women. On the other hand, vulnerability has been assigned to groups of people who lack the capacity for self-protection or for developing resilience or effective coping strategies (see Parrott et al, 2008). Moore and Miller (1999, p 1034), for example, propose vulnerability is associated with those who 'lack the ability to make personal life choices, to make personal decisions, to maintain independence and to self-determine.' With respect to health research with vulnerable service users, Pyer and Campbell (2013, p 154) refer to research participants who may have 'additional needs', including 'frail older people' as well as children and young people, people with mental health problems and learning difficulties. Using these kinds of classifications, we can see how groups of people with distinct needs, or those who experience particular challenges or difficulties, including people with learning difficulties, mental health problems, women victims-survivors of domestic violence, for example, have been categorised collectively as vulnerable.

In many respects, despite these definitional ambiguities and divergences, it is perhaps more relevant to understand vulnerability as a mutable concept, as well as a condition or circumstance to which people can become susceptible at any given time, depending on both their (unique, individual or systemic) circumstances and needs. For some people, being categorised as vulnerable (conditionally, circumstantially) can help identify and determine strategies for how needs can be met to alleviate or prevent vulnerability in the long term, particularly in health and social care contexts. Some individuals or groups may more readily be defined as vulnerable because of their diverse needs and, when problems combine or coincide, some people may also be defined as 'doubly vulnerable'. As Moore and Miller (1999, p 1035) propose, 'Combinations of factors, such as physical disability experienced during older adulthood or altered physiological status experienced during childhood and adolescence may render individuals doubly vulnerable.'

Thus, for some people, being identified as 'vulnerable' in health and social care contexts can be beneficial because it serves as a route to services and support. However, while those identified as such may not object on this basis alone, it is also the case that self-perceptions of vulnerability may not always accord with those of others, or according to external identifiers or classifications. Steel (2001, p 1) acknowledges both the number of individuals and groups who are described as vulnerable by service providers, for example, as well as the fact that 'some of these people would not describe themselves as vulnerable or marginalised at all', and that self perceptions of vulnerability are both socially constructed and again, contextual – '[it depends on] where you are standing at the time, and in relation to who, or what' (Steel, 2001, p 1).

Additionally, as Steel further points out, vulnerability both as a concept and condition is also dependent on the perspectives of social groups who themselves may consider mainstream organisations, for example, as culturally marginal. Steel cites the example of Travellers who may consider the NHS as 'marginal to their culture' (2001, p 2). It is also the case when reflecting on research objectives, processes and relationships when working with vulnerable or marginalised populations that a researcher's own perceptions of the nature and extent of vulnerability among participants with whom they are working are influenced, and can even be transformed, by their own perceptions and understandings about participants' needs and competencies based on the relationships that develop in research over time.

Thus we can see that, on the one hand, definitions or concepts of vulnerability may be helpful in certain contexts as protective or supportive mechanisms, as well as the fact that some people may experience vulnerability in more direct ways (when they have sensory impairments or experience chronic pain, for example; for a full discussion, see Chapter Three). On the other hand, *how* we define or conceptualise these difficulties, and as a consequence, the people who experience them, is an important consideration given that some people would not associate their problems or differences with vulnerability per se. Furthermore, the connotations associated with vulnerability and lack of self-reliance or need for beneficence are also problematic for some, in which case, research governance and ethical issues aside, it is helpful to understand vulnerability as a relative rather than an actual state or condition, which occurs as a result of external or structural factors and dynamics such as inequality and processes of social exclusion. It is in these ways – through the influence and effects, for example, of social injustice, discrimination and inequality – that people become powerless, excluded and marginalised. Different ways of understanding and re-conceptualising 'vulnerability' also enable us to understand the ways in which vulnerability and other forms of difference (such as disability and learning difficulty, for example) have become socially constructed.

These observations and issues are highlighted and discussed further in the chapters that follow. They also illustrate how reflexive considerations and practices in research can engender different perspectives on vulnerability, as well as on research processes and relationships and their relevance to professional practice. Equally, they also tell us something about PR with respect to relationship building, understanding and mutuality in instructive ways – as indeed they should. Otherwise, it could be argued that reflexive processes are reduced simply to exercises in self-indulgence (see Pillow, 2003, and the further discussion on reflexivity in Chapter Five).

Vulnerability and research ethics

Despite these important considerations, from a research governance and ethical perspective, individual self-perceptions of vulnerability or marginalisation, and philosophical and conceptual debates about them, are unimportant; what is important is that research participants themselves are not put at further risk of harm or their vulnerability exacerbated by research processes, and that researchers and institutions are equally protected. Thus, research governance frameworks and ethical guidelines provide extensive guidance about the type and extent of ethical clearance required in order for research studies that include vulnerable or marginalised groups to proceed (DH, 2005; ESRC, 2010, 2012).

However, the identifiers and classifications for vulnerable individuals and groups are, once again, somewhat broad here. For example, the Department of Health's (2005) *Research governance framework for health and social care* emphasises participants' capacity and willingness to provide informed consent as well as describes vulnerable or potentially vulnerable participants as children and adults with mental health problems or learning difficulties (2005, p 7). Economic and Social Research Council (ESRC) (2010, 2012) descriptors, on the other hand, focus on research that puts participants at 'more than minimal risk' and 'potentially vulnerable groups' as children and young people, those with learning difficulties or cognitive impairments, those who lack the mental capacity to give consent, and 'individuals in a dependent or unequal relationship' (p 8). Furthermore, and what is also particularly relevant to the research with the women victims-survivors of domestic violence (as well as victims of other forms of abuse or trauma) described in Chapter Three, research that focuses on 'sensitive topics' is also recognised as having the potential for creating or enhancing (existing) vulnerability among research participants. Of particular note in ESRC classifications here is research that collates evidence relating to participants' experiences 'of violence, abuse or exploitation' (2010, 2012, p 9). When taken together with research that might result in psychological distress to participants, as well as research that may require researchers to breach confidentiality because of harm or risk disclosures, it is perhaps easy to see how and why the parameters for vulnerability criteria are so broad from a research governance and ethical perspective.

While some researchers welcome the formal regulation of ethical procedures in the protection it affords participants, researchers and institutions (Munro, 2008), others have argued that stringent ethical procedures and requirements can, conversely, serve to exclude vulnerable or marginalised individuals and groups from being included in research studies (Boddy and Oliver, 2010; Hurdley, 2010; see also Hammersley 2010). Furthermore, as Steel (2001, p 1) notes, the range of individuals and groups who could be considered or categorised as vulnerable is 'very large', and this may be unhelpful or challenging to the extent that some individuals or groups may be excluded entirely from research studies on this basis alone. All of these issues and debates are pertinent both to the types of studies discussed in this and other chapters of this book as well as, more specifically, to the research projects described in Chapters Two, Three and Four that focus specifically on vulnerable/marginalised populations (for example, 'multiply vulnerable' children and young people, people with learning difficulties and women victims-survivors of domestic violence), as well as different concepts and interpretations of 'voice'. While I discuss the particular issues and challenges of involving and engaging with these kinds of vulnerable/ marginalised participants in research in more detail in the chapters that follow, it is important to emphasise here that in both research governance and ethical terms, these specific groups are considered vulnerable for a range of different reasons and according to a number of indicators.

Children and young people under the age of 18 who are also carers and people with learning difficulties are categorised as vulnerable either because of their circumstances or the nature of their illness/disability, or both. Women who have experienced domestic violence are considered or defined as vulnerable because of their victimised status, and their susceptibility to harm (physical and/or emotional), and in many instances, because of their lack of capacity for self-determination or autonomy. In addition, such women are also involved in unequal (power imbalanced) relationships when they experience abuse and intimidation from their partners or former partners. Domestic violence is also a highly sensitive topic, and very often research with women victims-survivors will involve revelations of abuse and violence that may not otherwise have been disclosed, and may also involve safeguarding or child protection issues and thus require breaches of confidentiality. Without careful adherence to ethical procedures, including confidentiality, consent and participant safety procedures, such vulnerable/marginalised participants could also be put at greater risk of harm by engaging in the research process itself. I discuss these ethical issues in more detail in the chapters that follow.

Participation, vulnerability and 'voice'

While vulnerability may be a contested and mutable concept in many respects, and while definitions vary depending on context and perspective, as outlined above, what underpins current understanding about vulnerability and its relevance to PR are notions of equality (or inequality) and power (or powerlessness). Thus, what is central to the relevance of, and relationship between, the participatory project and research with vulnerable or marginalised people – both in terms of research processes and outcomes – is the intention to address inequality and powerlessness by giving 'voice' to individuals who may be marginalised or excluded. Furthermore, as has been stated, such individuals are often denied full participation in public or political life and can be overlooked in research studies that adopt more conventional, non-PR approaches simply because they are deemed hard to access or to recruit onto research projects themselves (see Aldridge, 2012b).

Underpinning most PR approaches, then, in the social sciences (as well as in other fields and disciplines) is the notion of 'voice', which places the experiences of participants centre stage in research agendas and processes by enabling them to speak or 'tell' their individual or collective stories in their own ways or in ways that are deemed most appropriate to each individual or group. Notably, 'voice' in this context can be understood and interpreted in a number of different ways, theoretically, culturally and politically, as well as in (different) research methods and practices themselves (the visual 'voice', the narrative 'voice', for example). Thus, researchers keen to promote the voices of vulnerable or marginalised participants in research adopt a range of qualitative techniques such as life history research, interviewing, focus groups, diary and visual methods, and so on. In Thomson's (2008, p 3) research with children and young people, for example, visual methods are used in order to 'find ways to bring previously unheard voices into scholarly and associated professional conversations.' Acknowledging Britzman's (1989) multi-conceptual understanding of 'voice' (literal, metaphorical and political), Thomson recognises the importance generally of conferring competency and agency on vulnerable/marginalised research participants – of 'giving voice to the voiceless' (Britzman, 1989) – by engaging with them in more direct and inclusive ways using less conventional methods. For both Thomson and her colleagues, the use of participatory visual research methods presents valuable opportunities for involving children as the co-producers of research – by giving them cameras, video equipment, art materials and so on in order to collect their own evidence (see also Kaplan, 2008; Leitch, 2008; Noyes, 2008; for a further discussion about these methods specifically, see Chapter Two).

Other participatory methods which have also borrowed techniques from visual sociology, for example, in order to enhance participants' visual 'voice' and to work more inclusively with marginalised participants, combine the visual with first-person oral or written accounts, and introduce, for example, photographic diaries, PhotoVoice techniques and photographic elicitation methods (see Chapters Two and Three; see also Sempik et al, 2005; Aldridge and Sharpe, 2007; Joanou, 2009; Catalani and Minkler, 2010; Aldridge, 2012a). The intention here is not just to uncover new insights into lived experience that other more conventional methods might be less sensitive to, but also to generate greater understanding and more empathic *responses* – from the audience/reader as well as the researcher – to the visual narratives or 'voices' of vulnerable/marginalised participants.

Rapport's (2008, p 1) in-depth 'research conversation' with survivors of the Holocaust is a good example of this kind of empathic testimonial approach. Rapport used a combination of poetic (textual) and photographic narrative methods in order to take both the reader and the researcher on a textual-visual journey. Her objective – congruent with concepts of understanding and mutuality in research (see Bourdieu, 1996) – was to develop greater in-depth understanding of the researcher–participant relationship as well as research processes, including in the final output and communication phase. She describes these revelatory aspects of the study as a process of 'coming to know' the data, and argues that this approach makes visible 'what is often invisible in more traditional approaches' (Bourdieu, 1996). Indeed, the combination of the visual and the prose or poetic-style of the personal survivor narratives are both compelling and engender an emotional as well as empathic response that may be missed by other more conventional methods. The photograph of the barracks and execution wall at Auschwitz, for example, with its austere and imposing red brick façade and enclosed dirt yard, taken by Rapport herself, coupled with the personal narratives of the survivors, are compelling and intuitive testimonials of the survivor experience.

Narrative 'voice'

Congruent with the focus on PR in the last few decades and the recognition of the need for research to be more inclusive and individualised (even subjective) with respect to marginalised populations, is what has been termed the 'narrative moment' or the 'narrative turn'. Writing in the early 1990s, Richardson noted and welcomed the 'postmodernist climate' (1994, p 517) that both opened up and introduced new methods of enquiry and discourses, such as those described above, so that 'literary studies are about sociological questions; social scientists write fiction ... choreographers do sociology and so on' (Richardson, 1994, p 517). Plummer (1995) recognised this shift in disciplines such as anthropology, psychology, history and so on, describing it as the 'narrative moment', which facilitated and indeed encouraged closer focus on individualised, subjective accounts in qualitative research, and the development of methodologies that fostered a 'bottom-up', even case-by-case approach (Cornwall and Jewkes, 1995; Goodley and Moore, 2000).

In general terms, narrative research is defined broadly and simply as that which produces and analyses stories that are significant in people's lives (see Centre for Narrative Research, 2014), and that can also help to generate social change in a range of diverse contexts. Goodson (2013, p 4) for example, refers to the 'potential of stories, and the narrative techniques underpinning our storied existence, in particular their relationship to different social contexts and varying social purposes.' Within these broad parameters, knowledge production through the recalling and recounting of lived experience is placed centre stage in empirical processes.[1]

Thus, the representation of human experience as translated through personal stories or narratives – in written, spoken, visual form and so on – are also recognised increasingly as valuable and compelling in both evidential and practice terms (Fraser, 2004; Baldwin, 2013). And it is this facility in narrative research for creativity and to embrace different approaches and to cross-disciplinary boundaries that also offers real opportunities for more genuine participatory empirical endeavours. There are, therefore, a number of advantages in using these kinds of narrative approaches in PR studies with vulnerable or marginalised individuals and groups: the emphasis on personal representation (Goodson, 2013) places participants centre stage as the narrators/ tellers of stories (and thus embraces concepts of 'voice', of participatory 'voice'). Narrative approaches allow for methodological flexibility and creativity, particularly in qualitative research, and can facilitate different interpretations of 'voice' – through life history narratives, diary accounts, visual and visual-textual methods, for example. Furthermore, because of its emphasis on the significance of individualised discourses/ narratives, narrative research presents real opportunities for addressing inequality or powerlessness among vulnerable/marginalised participants whose voices are less likely to be heard.

The potential of small-scale narrative approaches in terms of research praxis is reflected and described in some of the participatory projects discussed in the following chapters of this book, but are made clear more specifically in the participatory narrative research project with women victims-survivors of domestic violence described in Chapter Four. In addition to the ways in which these types of participatory methods are used in research, narrative techniques are also used increasingly in education, health and social care practice, not just as a way of putting the spotlight on and advancing social pedagogy and developing professional practice, but, as Baldwin argues, also as a way of understanding 'the individual and the individual's relationship to society, through policy development and analysis' (2013, p 4; see the further discussion in Chapter Five).

However, despite Baldwin's assertion, it is also the case that both PR and narrative research also share similar challenges, particularly with respect to the extent to which they are accredited validity and credence in terms of the contributions they can make to the wider arena of evidence-based social policy, for example (see Walker et al, 2008). While these challenges have, to a large extent, been reflected in past debates about the differences between quantitative- and qualitative-based evidence, it can be seen that the same challenges faced by those working in the field of narrative research that relate to the need for greater methodological rigour and consistency (and particularly in research that uses small-scale, individualised narratives) are equally relevant to PR. Thus, the call Goodson makes (2013, p i) for narrative research to be more 'reliably structured' can also apply to PR and PR methods in many respects. Indeed, with respect to PAR, for example, Chevalier and Buckles argue (2013, p 5):

> More work and creativity is needed to strengthen the theoretical foundations of PAR, and chart a path of methodological innovation and authenticity. Theory matters and makes a difference in the methods chosen and the way real-life research is conducted.

Models of participatory research

As has been stated, there is considerable diversity in terms of the extent to which research projects that lay claim to participatory principles are genuinely inclusive – as Cornwall and Jewkes argue, 'while some conventional research projects involve limited interactions with people, others achieve a high level of in-depth participation, at certain stages, without being considered participatory' (1995, p 1668) – as well as whether or the extent to which projects give 'voice' to, and work effectively with, vulnerable or marginalised populations. Furthermore, PR projects may subscribe to inclusive and collaborative ideals and objectives, as well as recognise the effects of power imbalances in research processes and relationships, but other factors may undermine these priorities, both from the perspective of participants themselves and from those of researchers whose location or place in the academy may mean that their research priorities and objectives are influenced or constrained by other concerns or dilemmas (for example, professional drivers, the needs or priorities of funders; see Aldridge, 2012b). Thus, it is perhaps more appropriate and relevant to understand and describe PR along a continuum, but with specific reference to existing and developing participatory frameworks, models or typologies (see also Chapter Six), not just as a way of providing guidance to researchers who are planning PR projects, but also, and importantly, because such measures are necessary in order to lend greater clarity and rigour to PR methods and approaches.

With respect to existing models of PR, in their review of participatory methodologies in the mid-1990s, Cornwall and Jewkes referred to Biggs's (1989) four modes of participation (drawn from agricultural research) including contractual, consultative, collaborative and collegiate participation. For Biggs, *contractual participation* involves a simple arrangement in the researcher–'researched' relationship whereby participants are contracted into studies in order to extract data; participants engaged in the *consultative* mode are involved in consultation processes about research projects prior to their implementation; the *collaborative* mode involves researchers and participants working together in research processes, although projects are designed and managed by researchers themselves; and the *collegiate* mode is fully consultative and inclusive, with an emphasis on mutuality in terms of the planning, management and ownership of the research project (and is thus more congruent with PAR and 'emancipatory' approaches). Summarising these and other participatory models, Cornwall and Jewkes offer further refinements, referring to both 'shallow' participation, '[where] researchers control the entire process', and 'deep' participation, where 'there is movement towards relinquishing control and developing ownership of the process to those whom it concerns' (1995, p 1669).

Similarly, acknowledging the diversity in participatory projects, and designed as a starting point for researchers considering PR with children, Hart devised the Ladder of Participation model in which seven typologies or stages of PR were described that included 'manipulation' at the bottom of the ladder, where participants in research 'do or say what adults suggest they do. They have no real understanding of the issues, although they may be asked for their views. They do not know what influence their views will have on any decisions that are made' (1992, p 8; see also Steel, 2001). At the top of the ladder, research projects are initiated and directed by participants themselves (similarly, Hill's categories of participation with respect to research with children and young people makes distinctions between 'latent-participation [being present]' and 'active participation' as well as between 'piecemeal' and 'segregated' participation and fully integrated; 2006, p 73).

Although Hart has subsequently stated (2008, p 19) that the participatory Ladder was only ever intended as a 'jumping-off point' for researchers' own reflections on participatory approaches, such models are useful, if not, indeed, necessary, in order for researchers to align themselves and their research with a participatory agenda and to locate their research at some point on the PR scale (or 'ladder', in this case). Furthermore, they provide useful strategies for reflection, for considering the ways in which different participatory methods are able to address power imbalances in research relationships, and particularly when working with people defined or categorised as vulnerable (the Participatory Model described in Chapter Six, Figure 6.1, has been developed with these principles and objectives in mind). Such models or frameworks are also helpful in terms of promoting the opportunities for PR in equalising these relationships and in giving 'voice to the voiceless' (Thomson, 2008, p 3) – in order to make more concrete the relevance of PR for working more appropriately and collaboratively (both individually and collectively) with vulnerable or marginalised populations.

For researchers planning PR projects, then, it is necessary not only to locate their research at a point somewhere on the participatory 'ladder' or within a recognised participatory framework or model (despite the advances in PR, it is still the case that projects that lay claim to a participatory approach do not necessarily identify or describe the ways in which this is achieved or worked through), but also to reflect on the needs of their participants and how best to address and attempt to resolve inequality or powerlessness through inclusive and collaborative PR methods. It is only through careful reflection on the needs of participants, the nature of their vulnerability or marginalisation (whether this is innate, circumstantial or both, for example), as well as considering what is possible in terms of the type and extent of the participatory approach and through learning from other PR endeavours (including the benefits and challenges therein), that researchers can begin to lay claim to or align themselves genuinely with a PR approach.

It is important to note, of course, that in some cases the nature of participants' vulnerability (whether innate, circumstantial or multi-dimensional) can influence and even undermine PR objectives – and particularly at the 'emancipatory' or 'top end' of the Participatory Model (see Chapter Six, Figure 6.1) – and the ability of researchers to realise their collaborative or inclusive aspirations. To give an example here, PR with vulnerable/marginalised participants, by its very nature, often demands a high degree of flexibility and adaptability depending on the circumstances, status and needs of participants involved. As discussed in more detail in Chapter Three later, researchers working with people with learning difficulties, for example (defined as innately or uniquely vulnerable in research governance and ethics terms as well as in health and social care discourses) may intend to engage participants at the 'emancipatory' level, whereby they are involved collaboratively, and even as self-advocates, at all stages of the research process. However, depending on the nature or severity of the learning difficulty, some participants may not be able to understand or grasp concepts of research design, ethical issues, consent, and so on, because of limited cognitive capacity. While it is the case that PR methods in such instances would need to be both flexible and even, indeed, 'bespoke' – for example, using individualised, 'bottom-up' approaches (Goodley and Moore, 2000) – in order to achieve genuinely collaborative objectives, this may require proactive research strategies that are beyond the scope or timescale of some research projects and thus serve to undermine their participatory aims and principles.

Furthermore, perhaps a logical conclusion of any truly 'emancipatory' research agenda (for example, research that is located at the 'top end' of the Participatory Model) would underplay, if not deny completely, the role and 'voice' of the researcher as 'expert'. This could potentially mean that the reader or audience is left only with subjective, individual representations of lived experience. This may be advantageous in many respects, particularly in research studies where the intention is to challenge fixed perceptions (of disability, for example; see Aldridge, 2007) or stereotypes, or to revitalise or strengthen community action for example. On the other hand, we may simply be left with artistic impression only, in the case, say, of purely participatory visual narratives or presentations, in which the objective is simply emotive or sensory, rather than being socially or politically motivated in any way. An example here is Raine's (1994, p 16) visual project that looked at the production of home movies. Focusing on visual interpretations of home life through the use of video, Raine concluded, 'I don't want people to worry about whether it's true or whether it's fiction, I just want them to kind of live in this work – enter it, exist in it, enjoy it.' While laudable in many respects, these kinds of approaches can be especially problematic if participants and researchers aren't involved collaboratively on projects, including during analysis and outputs phases, and particularly in the context of social policy research, where evidence from social research studies is used to shape both policy and practice.

While some researchers, in adopting a participatory approach, do not wrestle with these tensions intentionally, simply choosing instead to 'get on with facilitating the co-investigation' (Chevalier and Buckles, 2013, p 38), when using participatory methods with vulnerable or marginalised groups in social policy research, for example, many would argue that the role and expertise of researchers even at the 'emancipatory' level should not simply be overlooked or denied. Indeed, both in methods terms and in terms of research outcomes, in many respects there is a distinct role for the researcher to contribute to the production and advancement of knowledge – including in emancipatory, 'top-end' PR approaches – either through jointly communicating the messages from research to policy makers and practitioners, for example, advancing academic debates about methods, ethics and research praxis, or through representation when participants are unable to represent themselves or influence social change (see Chapter Five for a more detailed discussion on this point). For the researcher planning or engaged in PR with vulnerable/marginalised participants there is, of course, a degree of tension in the interplay between the different roles and responsibilities they must adopt and address if they are to treat research as 'a distinct profession' while at the same time promote participation and inclusion in research praxis at the 'emancipatory' level (see Aldridge, 2012b).

Participatory research in broader, social and political contexts

It is clear that individualised, bottom-up approaches in PR are both appropriate and necessary when working with vulnerable participants in research, and such strategies are also congruent with more recent shifts in other disciplines and methodologies that have witnessed a move from the 'grand narratives' of the past, 'of human intention and progress' (Goodson, 2012, p 10), to small-scale narratives which embrace individualised 'meaning making' and subjectivity (p 4). However, such approaches are not always sympathetic to the social change objectives that should and do underpin much of PR, and PAR specifically, or necessarily with the requirements of policy makers, for example (see Walker et al, 2008). Participatory and PAR approaches in particular are underpinned distinctly (and philosophically) by transformative objectives. Park (1993, p 2), for example, argues that PR should engender social justice transformations. Walmsley and Johnson (2003, p 29) also propose that PAR should demonstrate 'a commitment to structural social change designed to create a more just and equitable society.' Of course, in many respects, the degree to which change occurs as a result of new evidence from participatory studies is also dependent on a number of factors that are not only influenced by research objectives and processes (methodological choice, research design, and so on), as is illustrated in Walmsley and Johnson's further claim that effective outcomes in PAR are the responsibility of both researchers *and* participants.

One of the further aims of PAR projects is that they involve and have positive transformative outcomes at a *local* or *community* level. However, once again, where the need for participatory approaches in research is influenced and determined by the needs of vulnerable or marginalised individuals and groups, and particularly multiply vulnerable participants, then it is likely that some of these will also be socially excluded or difficult to identify or access, and may also not be part of any identifiable or known 'community'. Thus, while an individualised, bottom-up PR approach would be necessary in order to identify, access and work effectively with such participants, the transformative opportunities and facility for generating social change at a collective or community level may be compromised simply by the lack of collective 'voice' or community representation, and thus a 'credible' evidence base from which such change can be implemented (in social policy and practice terms). Therefore, there are a number of obvious tensions between an individualised PR approach, and community-based social or structural change objectives. As Cornwall and Jewkes (1995, p 1673) also note, 'even when researchers find a discrete community, they need to be cautious of coherent expressions of "community" needs or priorities, "we think…", "we want…" may reflect a significant distortion of individuals' aspirations.'

Thus, in terms of the role and responsibility of the PR researcher and the transformative nature of PR – particularly that which involves working with vulnerable/marginalised groups in social policy research, for example – the individualised narrative, the 'realist tale', or the life history or personal testimony needs to be presented and understood both contextually and collectively (one question might be, for example, how and what does the individual participatory narrative, story or account contribute to wider evidence and knowledge?) as well as provide clear directional and impact objectives for participants and for research praxis. In PR, where there is a greater degree of role transference and where participants can become not only co-researchers but also the authoritative 'voices' in research, the direction and objectives of the research need to be made clear in order to avoid ambiguity about ownership and the degree to which participants as authors can influence the transformative elements of such research (see the further discussion in Chapters Five and Six).

The collective participatory 'voice'

Perhaps one of the most significant challenges for social policy researchers in achieving some of these objectives lies in addressing and reconciling the need to 'collectivise' evidence based on an individualised approach (or, put another way, the need to 'objectivise' the subjective). For researchers engaged in, and committed to, a participatory agenda, one of the ways of addressing inequality in research relationships and facilitating participant autonomy and voice is to design and conduct research at the 'top end' or 'emancipatory' level in PR (see Chapter Six, Figure 6.1). However, at the same time, researchers need to ensure that evidence from PR projects contributes new understanding and insights about social issues or problems, for example, in order to bring about change. For the PR researcher engaged in more collaborative research with vulnerable or marginalised individuals (and particularly those who are multiply vulnerable, marginalised and isolated), this can present a real challenge, but it is one that must be addressed. In some cases researchers themselves will be required to aggregate and systematise individualised data (based on disparate individual life stories or narratives) in order to provide a 'convincing' evidence base or contribute new knowledge. This process – that essentially rests and relies on the professionalised role of the researcher – may or may not involve research participants themselves as co-researchers. As has been stated previously (and is discussed in more detail in the proceeding chapters), it may not always be possible to work exclusively at the 'emancipatory' level in PR.

Furthermore, with respect to the broader roles and responsibilities of researchers (including to funders and to the academy, for example), despite the many advances in PR and emancipatory research, it is still the case that the onus most often falls on academic researchers to collect, analyse and interpret research data, including those based on individualised, personal accounts from small numbers of cases, in order to contribute new insights into *existing* bodies of research and knowledge (see Simons, 2009). In the context of PR, it is also the responsibility of researchers to ensure that there is greater collaboration in these processes. From a PAR perspective, Chevalier and Buckles (2013, p 5) refer to this as 'scaling up' the investigative process:

> This requires that we develop and use more advanced techniques to shore up the PAR contribution to evidential reasoning and dialogue. Instead of scaling down the inquiry process to quick-and-easy conversations between the parties involved, PAR practitioners must make sure the questions asked and methods used do justice to the pressing issues at hand, the richness of participant knowledge and local views about the matters under investigation, *and the broader lessons from research and field-specific knowledge.* (emphasis added)

Some examples of individual 'voices' and collective stories

The research projects described and discussed in Chapters Two, Three and Four show how personal, individualised narratives in social policy research have helped to inform and shape broader public and political discourses, as well as influence and transform social policies and the lives of participants themselves. With respect to research with vulnerable children and young people – and young carers specifically – as discussed in Chapter Two, the examples here reveal the ways in which children and young people's voices have contributed new knowledge at a time when broader social, cultural and political discourses began to focus on what has been described as the 'narrative of the mind' of children (see Hendrick, 2003).

This shift in perception of childhood and children's status as the 'knowers' and 'tellers' of lived experience is reflected more generally in the growing numbers of qualitative research studies on childhood and children's individual experiences. As Hill notes (2006, p 72), 'In recent years there has been an explosion of consultation and of qualitative research with children and young people [which] reflects a number of influences, including the growth of a participatory rights perspective and of social studies of childhood.' Described in further detail in Chapter Two, the specific example of research on young caring reflects both this broader interest in, and assimilation of, children's voices in research, policy and practice discourses. It also shows the ways in which 'broader lessons' from (participatory) research (Chevalier and Buckles, 2013, p 5) can also help to bring about social change through the weight of evidence about new social issues or problems (in this case, for young carers and their families themselves).

Research on people with learning difficulties has been informed and developed as a result of new approaches to disability research and activism (starting in the mid-1970s; see Tregaskis, 2002) that moved away from a strictly medical model to a social model of disability, which served as a catalyst for both political and social change. This shift also presented researchers with new ways of working with people with disabilities, including those with learning difficulties, which emphasised consultation and collaboration (see Booth, 1996; Goodley and Moore, 2000). Nind (2008, p 5) states that people with learning difficulties are 'calling for greater say in research that is about them', and at the same time proposes that this has resulted in policy makers recognising this need. Nevertheless, conducting research with people with learning difficulties presents a number of ethical and practical challenges that have and could continue to mean they are excluded or overlooked in research – including research that lays claim to participatory objectives – precisely because of these barriers (see Aldridge, 2012b). These issues are explored and discussed in Chapter Three in order to demonstrate the ways in which PR approaches can help to overcome some of these challenges.

Thus, new advances in disability research and research on and with children and young people has increased our knowledge and understanding of the experiences and needs of these groups, and has led to a number of important social and political changes. The same is also true now in terms of our understanding about women's experiences of domestic violence (discussed in more detail in Chapter Four). We knew very little about this social problem until the 1970s with impetus from the women's movement, feminism and women's activism and campaigning as well as research that included the voices of women victims and survivors themselves (see Ellsberg and Heise, 2005). Now, as Romito (2008, p 1) argues, 'Violence against women and children is no longer a secret, something that the victims have to hide, without hope and without means of release. We are more and more aware of the frequency and consequences of domestic violence....' Of course, finding the courage to speak up – to tell their stories in the first place, to have a 'voice' – and know that they will be believed, as well as the impact of the abuse itself, are still issues that present significant challenges to women who experience domestic violence (see Seeley and Plunkett, 2002; Banyard, 2010; Aldridge, 2013).

However, without women's individual stories and voices in research, in political debate and in practice, alongside women's activism and campaigning, we would have no evidence or *collective* testimony from which to make sense of or analyse the experiences of women who have been and continue to be abused by their partners or former partners. What is important in research (and practice) terms is that the discourse on domestic violence – seen very much, and importantly, through the lens of feminism – has been shaped by women's individual stories, but also continues to help shape new and ongoing narratives as well as analytical and interpretative processes at (and, indeed, in) both the micro and macro level (Haaken, 2010; Allen, 2011; Aldridge, 2013). Furthermore, taken together, the *collective* evidence on domestic violence and the reality of its impacts on women from their perspectives are both compelling and highly resistant to refutation or claims against validity or credibility.

Conclusion

This chapter has considered the benefits, and challenges, of PR and its relevance to working with vulnerable or marginalised individuals and groups. It has been noted that not all PR studies, even those that aim to engage with vulnerable participants specifically, adopt methods and procedures that are genuinely or at all times empathic and participatory in nature (see Aldridge, 2012b). Furthermore, some participants are marginalised or 'hard to reach' to such an extent that individualistic or 'case-by-case' methods are required (see Goodley and Moore, 2000), and these approaches can be particularly time-consuming and challenging ethically, and can serve to compromise social change objectives. While the advantages of a more coherent alliance between PR approaches and working with vulnerable groups are clear, a number of other challenges also present themselves, not just in the mechanics or performance of such a convergence, but in the realisation of aspirations common to both in broader social, cultural and political contexts – in the difference perhaps between 'small' and 'grand narratives' (in narrative or life history research; see Goodson, 2013), and in ensuring the 'voices' of vulnerable people are heard beyond the boundaries of the PR project itself. As has been stressed, the difference also lies in using personal or individualised stories (in whatever form) to illustrate identity formation, selfhood and subjectivity, for example, among groups about which little is known (and that may be very difficult to access and include in research processes; see Aldridge, 2007), and research that aims to use evidence to bring about change and transform lives, particularly in the context of social policy research. As Walker and colleagues state (2008, p. 164), 'the world of policy and practice tends to be more cautious in its response' to this type of evidence.

A further challenge for social research studies that use less conventional methods such as PR and PAR (and including narrative representations) therefore lies in reconciling the need for faithful demonstration or representation of lived experience (particularly of vulnerable or marginalised groups who might otherwise be left out of research studies) and the need to inform wider audiences. While the processes of individualised storytelling or narrative construction are important considerations alongside the subjective interpretations of the narrators themselves, these should not be considered as either separate from or disaffected by broader contextual issues. As Fraser (2004, p 182) has argued, through her use of narrative or storytelling methods in social work practice, such approaches are only ever 'escapist' if they ignore broader social and political dimensions.[2] While it is undoubtedly the case that participatory objectives and priorities (in both methods and practice terms) can and do lead to greater understanding about needs and are congruent with a much-valued (and vaunted) rights-based social and political agenda, these outcomes can also be compromised by inconsistent or piecemeal approaches to participation, by a lack of appropriate resources in order to facilitate or improve consultation processes, for example (see Hill et al, 2004), and by a lack of understanding about the needs of vulnerable or socially excluded people.

A further consideration in PR and PAR with vulnerable or marginalised individuals and groups is that methods used should be, as Walker and colleagues further state, 'high in credibility', as well as 'provide clear directions for policy and practice' (2008, p 164). For these authors, the solution lies in using participatory approaches to serve as catalysts for negotiating new meanings and directions in organisations that are undergoing change, for example, as well as to use these methods to try and disrupt prevailing power dynamics and relationships (see the further discussion in Chapter Five).

The point about providing clear direction for policy and practice is a pertinent one, however, and returns us in part to the need for greater conceptual clarity regarding the relationship between PR and vulnerability, as well as empirically with respect to the types of participatory methods used, and the location of research projects within a coherent PR framework or model. Such considerations are important to the PR debate, especially as it is suggested by some that more creative, personalised and less conventional research methods often lack the 'accepted norms and standards' for presenting data that are available for other more traditional methods (see Poindexter, 2002, p 713). It is perhaps also helpful, therefore, to consider PR not as contingent but as continua, that is, PR methods need to evolve and develop according to coherent and realistic research objectives and agendas and the commitment of researchers (as the originators and designers of research projects) to participatory and emancipatory agendas.[3]

Having acknowledged the number of issues and challenges confronting the PR researcher, it is nonetheless encouraging that in recent years more emphasis has been placed in social research studies on the voices of vulnerable, marginalised groups that facilitate new opportunities in PR and PAR, and to develop and advance new emancipatory agendas. At the same time, recognition has been given to the existence and influence of power dynamics in researcher–researched relationships and ways of addressing and overcoming these dynamics through the emphasis on 'voice'. In their discussion of the power of the student voice in education research, Arnot and Reay (2007, p 314) recognise, for example, that developing methods in post-structuralist and post-modern research 'use voice as indicative of subjectivity and power, distinguishing "between the dominant voice and those ('Others') silenced or marginalised by its hegemony"…(Moore and Muller, 1999, p 190).' Such power dynamics can be even less marked if and when participants are engaged more directly and collaboratively in PR projects (Centre for Narrative Research, 2011; Walmsley and Johnson, 2003), therefore, in approaches where the participants in research are more than just sources of data, but are active in research processes themselves, as evidenced in the examples of PR projects discussed in the chapters that follow. Nevertheless, despite the fact that the evidence for working more collaboratively with vulnerable or marginalised participants in these ways is convincing, a number of important ethical considerations and challenges also present themselves in these contexts, and it is to these and related issues that I also turn in the following chapters.

TWO

Participatory research with children and young people

Recognising and including children and young people in research, policy and practice

In her work on children's roles and representation in social research in the mid-1990s, Alderson (1995, p 40) claimed that the views of children and young people had been generally overlooked in research studies. She described the 'adult-centred' nature of research until that time, which was 'conducted about the public world of the environment, politics, economics and other social affairs with little reference to children.' Others have made similar observations, claiming also that one of the main reasons children have been marginalised in society for so long is because of the absence of their authentic voices in public discourses about childhood (Brown, 1998; Hill et al, 2004). Indeed, in 2004 (prior to the start of a series of national seminars on children and young people's participation in research, policy and practice in the UK), Hill and colleagues argued that children were one of the most highly governed groups in society, and that lack of recognition for their competence and agency had 'confined them to a state of impotency' (p 84).

However, recent developments – theoretically, empirically and in policy and practice – that aim to address children's marginalisation and exclusion from society subscribe to a new agenda of enhancing children's participation in public and political life so that they are more directly involved in decisions that affect them. These developments are underpinned by a rights-based approach to children and young people's experiences and needs with reference to principles of participation that are underscored by an international mandate (United Nations [UN] *Convention on the Rights of the Child*; see UNICEF, 1989, Article 12; see also International Save the Children Alliance, 2008). Theoretically they are also aligned to the 'new' sociology of childhood that sees children as active citizens with important contributions to make (see Wyness, 2006; see also Mayall, 2002). These issues are explored in this chapter with reference to new and developing research methods that enhance children's participation and work directly with them to facilitate children's voices in research. Particular attention is given to research on young carers in the UK, which started in the early 1990s, and demonstrates how new approaches to working inclusively with vulnerable children and young people can result in social and political transformations as well as improve their quality of life and the lives of their families.

Constructing and re-constructing childhood

It has been argued that children and young people have unique insights to offer, about specific aspects of their childhood and teenage years, and about the phase of childhood more generally, and that without these insights a distorted and unrepresentative picture is presented which can and does have adverse consequences for how children are perceived and treated in society (see Franklin, 2002; Thomson, 2008). An example here is the way in which children and young people have been represented publicly, and specifically, in media narratives that focus on children and young people 'as risk' – those who present a 'threat' to society and social order through their anti-social and offending behaviour.[1] It is argued that these kinds of representations of childhood have been produced and reproduced by adult journalists and media professionals in public discourses and contexts, with little or no consultation or direct communication with children and young people themselves, or reference to the causes of children's anti-social or offending behaviour – for example, how social exclusion has an impact on their lives (see Franklin, 2002; Aldridge and Cross, 2008).

A further example is how, until relatively recently, the views and perceptions of children and young people have been overlooked in health research on 'families'. It has only been in the last 30 years or so that the medical model of mental illness has, for example, if not been replaced with, then at least been reconsidered in light of, broader social ecological perspectives and the new family model that promote the views and perspectives of children as well as parents (see Falkov, 2013). Prior to this time, clinical and medical research considered children as largely at risk of developmental delay, physical harm and/or injury, and of contracting mental illness themselves when living with a first degree relative who had a diagnosed mental health problem (see Aldridge and Becker, 2003). Our understanding now about children's experiences of living in families affected by parental mental illness (as well as other illnesses and disabilities) has been improved by evidence from research studies that use methods that engage directly with children themselves about their needs. As a consequence we have a greater social and ecological understanding about mental illness and its implications for family life (see Aldridge, 2006; Mordoch and Hall, 2008; Falkov, 2013).

These developments have occurred as a result of, and alongside, the emergence of new cross-disciplinary perspectives, methodologies and approaches in the social, health and other sciences more broadly (see the discussion earlier, in Chapter One). This, in turn, has resulted in greater convergence, particularly in recent years, between research and practice within (and across) disciplines, and particularly among both researchers and practitioners who want to work with vulnerable children and young people as participants, patients and service users in different, more inclusive and collaborative ways. As Hill (2006, p 72) argues:[2]

> There has been an increasing overlap between the two spheres, with both now encompassing a wide range from the highly informal to formal, with many variations and combinations in between. Certain agencies have carried out questionnaire surveys or sponsored interview studies [while] games, role play and exercises are now quite common in academic research, partly for interactional and partly for data gathering purposes.

Furthermore, in child and youth-related policy and practice in the UK there has also been greater recognition and inclusion of children and young people's views in recent years, underlining the participatory agenda and principles enshrined in an international rights-based approach to childhood (as evidenced in the UN *Convention on the Rights of the Child*; see UNICEF, 1989). An example here is the consultation with children and young people for the review and reform of children's services (launched by the then Labour government in 2003) that culminated in the *Every child matters* (ECM) (DfE, 2003) agenda. The five outcomes and principles of ECM were based on what children themselves said they needed, and as a consequence of this new participatory agenda, children and young people were also directly involved in the recruitment and appointment of a new Children's Commissioner for England in 2005. At that time, the government's commitment to consulting with, and listening to, children and young people was made concrete: 'It is intended that the Children's Commissioner will be a powerful "listening post" for children and young people, and an important part of the commitment to place children at the centre of reforms' (House of Commons Education and Skills Committee, 2004, p 16).

However, despite these new strategies and the new 'listening to children' agenda, it has been claimed that children's voices in public and political discourses are not prioritised in all areas of public and political life, and that to some extent their 'participation activities remain under-resourced' (Hill et al, 2004, p. 81), particularly among specific groups such as very young children and those who are chronically sick or disabled (thus, those categorised as multiply vulnerable). Furthermore, both then and now, aspects of children and young people's lives are beset with challenges and tensions that mean that not all children enjoy equal access to opportunity, choice and participation (nor, indeed, the five principles and objectives set out in the ECM agenda). For example, there are continuing tensions between the ways in which children's needs and rights are recognised in health, social care and welfare approaches to childhood, and in youth justice approaches specifically (see Aldridge and Cross, 2008). There are also clear tensions with respect to the children and citizenship agenda. While successive governments in the UK have made a commitment to citizenship rights for children through the continued inclusion of citizenship provision in schools and the national curriculum, as well as the Coalition government's introduction of the National Citizen Service (Gov.UK, 2013), critics of the children and citizenship agenda have suggested that it is either tokenistic or treats children simply as 'human capital' – 'children count not as child-citizens in the here and now but as citizen-workers of the future' (Lister, 2005, p 29).

Thus, despite more recent advances and shifts in perceptions about childhood and how children should be understood and treated, different areas of children's social, education, political and cultural lives remain fraught with tensions and contradictions, including the ways in which their needs and rights are represented and addressed (through children's health and social care services, youth justice interventions, media representations of children, and so on). Furthermore, it is only relatively recently that theoretical and epistemological understandings about children's needs and the phase of childhood itself have undergone some necessary transformations. In 1997, James and Prout referred to new (sociological) understandings about childhood as an 'emergent paradigm', and identified the 1990s as a time when the sociology of childhood 'was only just beginning to emerge as a distinct sub-discipline' (James and Prout, 2005, p vii). Prior to this time, dedicated sociological understandings of childhood tended not to take into account children's competency or agency; rather, they were seen predominantly as passive individuals to whom health and social care and education services were administered or delivered, or who underwent a process of socialisation, as well as different psychological stages, that meant children could be (and were) simply the objects *of* study (see Durkheim, 1961; Erikson, 1963; James et al, 1998).

Furthermore, while more contemporary understandings about children and young people have both recognised and incorporated different epistemologies, including the social construction of childhood, structural sociological perspectives and the 'new' sociology of childhood (see Alanen and Mayal, 2001), it is clear that these advances in knowledge and understanding are not always reflected in children's own experiences of childhood, in public perceptions and attitudes towards them, and in the type and extent of services and support offered to them. Research by the Child Poverty Action Group (CPAG), for example, has revealed that in terms of health, education and housing standards, the UK is one of the worst places in Europe for children to grow up, and that child poverty is predicted to rise considerably in the next five years as a result of austerity measures and welfare cuts (CPAG, 2013). In a Joseph Rowntree study of children's transitions into adulthood (Barry, 2001), the children and young people who took part said they did not have adequate information or support about living independently, felt discriminated against by parents and professionals who didn't understand their emotional or practical needs, and that they were also unaware of their rights.

Such tensions and contradictory messages about children's experiences and how they are perceived, represented and treated by adults in society are undoubtedly reflected in the duality that childhood represents – the knowledge and recognition that while children can and do make important contributions and can be competent and active 'citizens', at the same time in their daily lives they are inevitably susceptible to violence, abuse and victimisation (because they are children and thus relatively powerless), which renders them in need of protection. In policy and practice terms this has led to the development and introduction of numerous (and necessary) child protection and safeguarding policies over the years; with respect to research conducted on and with children and young people, it has also resulted in the development and advancement of new research governance and ethical frameworks (and guidance) that inevitably define children and young people under the age of 18 as vulnerable. However, it is these very issues that can present a number of challenges for researchers who work with or who plan to work with children and young people, and particularly when engaging with them in more inclusive ways through the use of PR methods.

Ethical considerations in research with children and young people

> In everyday social life, we (as adults, parents or researchers) tend not to be respectful of children's views and opinions and the challenge is to develop research strategies that are fair and respectful to the subjects of our research. (Morrow and Richards, 1996, p 91)

When Morrow and Richards made this proposition for working ethically with children in research, few studies up until this time used participatory methods that engaged directly with children or emphasised their agency and voice. As the authors themselves discuss, key concerns focused mainly on issues of consent, confidentiality and children's safety, and these have developed into more concrete ethical frameworks and guidelines since that time (see DH, 2004, 2005; NCB, 2004; Boddy and Oliver, 2010). Today, children and young people under the age of 18 are classified as vulnerable in research governance and ethics terms (as discussed earlier in Chapter One), and for reasons that inevitably reflect children's status in society (their relative powerlessness) and thus their need for protection from harm. Two decades ago, Lansdown (1994) referred to children's vulnerability as both inherent and structural, but which was also influenced by misconceptions about their lack of knowledge and experience. Lansdown and others called for different kinds of approaches that would enhance children's participation and at the same time contribute to the validity and rigour of evolving PR approaches (see also Thomas and O'Kane, 1998).

In her consideration of ethical requirements when working with children in research, Alderson suggested that an essential first step was to ensure that the research questions asked of children were both necessary and valid. Thomas and O'Kane also described important principles of research ethics that should involve children's 'active agreement' to participate, their right to withdraw, and choice (as far as possible) over the methods of participation (1998, p 339). These same ethical issues and principles remain pertinent today when working with children in research – indeed, with all vulnerable or marginalised groups. While we have moved beyond setting age thresholds for children's participation in research – indeed, this is one of the areas in which the development of PR methods and debates about participation have advanced ethical understanding and practices including children's capacity to give informed consent as well as 'informed dissent' (Morrow and Richards, 1996, p 95) – a number of key ethical prerequisites of working appropriately and safely with children and young people in research continue to be important.

Of particular importance here are issues of consent, confidentiality and dealing with disclosures and protection issues even though, as Christensen and Prout (2002, p 491) observe, there is sometimes 'disproportionate emphasis on these aspects of research',[3] when in fact, ethical issues and considerations should be seen as part of 'ongoing social practice'. In many respects, ethical considerations are reflected in the *if*, *why*, *how*, *where* and *when* of both research practice and praxis when working more directly with children and young people as part of an ongoing process of communication and dialogue (see Morrow and Richards, 1996; Christensen and Prout, 2002).

Processes of participation: children's involvement in research

Such processes involve giving children opportunities to participate (or not) in research on their own terms by building carefully negotiated relationships with them as well as discussing with them the implications of taking part and the kinds of participatory methods that are more suited to their needs. At these early stages in research studies, questions about whether the research itself and the research questions asked are necessary and valid can be confirmed, or otherwise, by children themselves. Children also require age-appropriate information about the research so that they can make informed decisions about whether they want to participate, can consider the benefits to themselves, or their families, of participation, and if they have the time and space in their lives to do so (thus avoiding assumptions that were often made in the past that one of the few benefits of involving children in research was because they have 'adequate free time') (Spradley, 1959, p 51).

In many respects, whether children choose to participate in research that is about them (the *if* in research practice involving children) may depend not on children's own choices, but the choices and decisions of others, and particularly those of adults involved in their lives. Mediators, advocates or 'gatekeepers' such as parents or health, social care or education professionals may intervene to make decisions on children's behalf about their participation in research. Indeed, some researchers have found that children's participation in research is sometimes denied based on spurious notions of what is in the best interests of children, without their ever being asked directly about their desire or willingness to be involved (see Heath et al, 2004; Masson, 2004).

These challenges are sometimes hard to avoid, particularly in participatory approaches that aim to engage with children in more direct and collaborative ways. In their longitudinal ethnographic study of children in early education in Italy, Corsaro and Molinari (2008) recognised that gaining membership status and insider perspectives on the children's lives at school relied on developing good relationships with 'gatekeepers' – in this case, school teaching staff, managers and parents who 'had varying degrees of control over our access to the research site and the activities of the children' (p 242). For the authors, successfully gaining access to children to participate in the research relied on effective negotiations with these 'gatekeepers', which in turn were determined by a number of factors, including the collaborative nature of the research methods, prior experience of working with the schools involved, and effective and ongoing communication with all staff and participants about the study and the findings that it generated (at both the interim and final stages of the project). This stage of the research was considered to be essential in establishing relationships of trust and rapport with all stakeholders and participants and in order for the authors to '[negotiate] through the bureaucracy of the Italian education system' (Corsaro and Molinari, 2008, p 242).

Whether children choose to participate in research that is about them (or whether they are allowed, or enabled, to make a choice), or if they choose to continue to participate throughout the duration of research studies or not, will also be dependent on how rigorously researchers observe and work with necessary child protection or safeguarding procedures. While mechanisms for dealing with issues of confidentiality and, specifically, children's disclosures of risk or harm, should be an essential prerequisite for working with children and young people under the age of 18 in research, adopting a genuinely participatory and child-centred approach will mean engaging in careful and ongoing dialogue with children themselves about these important issues, and establishing agreed procedures from the outset. For some researchers, this involves communicating with children about the consequences for them of disclosing risk or harm, and that such disclosures would need to be relayed to third parties in order to protect children from further harm, for example. For others, such an approach may represent a betrayal of children's trust or be seen as undermining their opportunities to speak freely and autonomously in research, in which case, researchers must attempt to reach a compromise between what, for them at least, may often be seen as opposing dynamics.

In their research on looked-after children, Thomas and O'Kane (1998), for example, adopted an approach that allowed the children who participated to speak freely, but they were also told from the outset that disclosures during interview would indicate to the researchers that the children were prepared for this information to be passed on to a third party whom the children trusted: 'if the information indicated that the child was being harmed, it would be our responsibility to support the child in telling someone who was in a position to do something about it; but this would have to be done with the child's consent' (p 340).

The need for strict measures to address disclosures of serious risk or harm to participants will also be more or less relevant depending on the nature and context of the research project concerned. In the context of research with children and young people, if the research is about highly sensitive topics such as child abuse or childhood trauma, for example, then disclosure strategies will be particularly pertinent, but less so if they focus on more generalised childhood experiences and perspectives, for example, attitudes to citizenship, friendships and so on.

How children participate in research – the methods and mechanisms for their participation – will be determined by the underlying principles and approaches of social research investigations (whether they are participatory or not, for example), as well as in the specifics, such as the methods and research tools and instruments used, and whether there is consultation with children about these. In many respects these matters are also determined by the age, gender, cultural background and so on of the intended research population, as well as a range of other factors that may be unique to individual children – when and where children can participate, for example, whether they have the space and time in their lives, and if not, how this might be facilitated to ensure their participation, if that is what they want.

Age is a critical factor in determining how children participate in research (and, indeed, whether they also take part) because not all research methods will be appropriate in terms of delineating the various needs of children at different stages of their development. However, age should not be regarded simply as a biological or chronological construct, but should also be considered in terms of children's level of maturity. Christensen and Prout (2002, p 483) further propose that children's ability to participate in research and to make important contributions as children should not simply be assessed on their age or stage of development, but that 'variations in children's social experiences and social competencies' should also be considered, 'by identifying the commonalities and differences between children in the particular contexts we research.' For some children and young people, however, their social and cultural experiences inevitably conflict with other aspects of their lives and their status and roles as children, and this is illustrated perfectly in the example of young carers – children whose level of maturity is often delineated by the nature and extent of their (caring) responsibilities, and which are not always congruent with their actual (biological or developmental) age (see the discussion below).

One of the reasons for involving children and young people themselves in discussions about how they wish to participate in research (in line with participatory objectives) from the outset is to recognise the distinction between 'childhood' as an age-delineated construct and how it is manifest in the experiences, perspectives and attitudes of individual children themselves. In many respects these issues are further complicated by the nature and extent of children's vulnerability and how difficult (or easy) they are to access and include using agreed methods. It may be that an individual, case-by-case methodological approach is necessary (using 'bespoke' methods) because of children's particular needs as well as the sensitive nature of the research topic; thus, in some cases, the methods used in research will be determined by the nature or extent of children's vulnerability, marginalisation or isolation. It may also be the case that some children are not part of a recognised group or community, and thus where and when they participate will be determined by their availability at a given time or location. For those children who haven't been involved in research before (and where the research focuses on a subject about which little is known), or who are not part of recognised group, then the methods used may need to focus on what Kitzinger (1994, p 116) describes as, 'individual biographies or the minutiae of decision making during intimate moments', rather than on methods that generate data on a large scale. In policy terms, however, one of the aims of PR should also focus on transforming these individual, in-depth stories from children (and other vulnerable individuals and groups) into collective evidence, or into what Lewis and Porter (2004, p 196) describe as the 'collective "choir"'.

Participatory research with children and young people

With respect to research that lays claim to a participatory agenda and objectives, it is important, then, that children are considered competent and autonomous in terms of their ability to participate fully in research processes, and yet, on the other hand, their vulnerability (innately, circumstantially, legally, and so on) also needs to be acknowledged and managed in practice. Thus, recognising children's potential vulnerability (to exploitation, risk, harm, etc) that is assigned to them by dint of their age and status (as children), and at the same time acknowledging their competency as potentially active citizens, presents the main challenges to PR. This duality can also mean that some researchers are averse to working with children and young people because of the perceived difficulties of gaining access to them (and especially to multiply vulnerable or marginalised individual children and young people), of engaging with them in accordance with strict ethical guidelines, and of including them in more direct ways using flexible and less conventional methods.[4]

To further complicate this issue, it is important to note that we cannot always assume that just because we as adults consider children's participation in research to be important philosophically, morally, ethically and so on, that children themselves will feel the same way. This is why it is vital that dialogue with children about their participation is seen as an essential and ongoing process in research, and through the use of different, even bespoke, methods of data collection. There are numerous examples of these new kinds of approaches that include the use of images and drawings by children, scrapbooks, video and photographic PR and peer research, as well as different creative methods with very young children (Clark and Moss, 2005; Aldridge and Sharpe, 2007; Bragg and Buckingham, 2008; Haw, 2008; Noyes, 2008; Walker et al, 2008; Joanou, 2009; NCAS, 2013). In peer research, for example, children and young people are involved at all stages of the research process and are included as co-researchers throughout. In the Right2BeCared4 project (NCAS, 2013) young care leavers interviewed other care leavers as part of the research study. One of the peer researchers involved in the project described this as 'the most motivating part ... knowing that through this, young people were given a voice, a chance to share their opinions on the transition from care to independent living' (p 6). A further example of children undertaking their own research studies is the work being carried out for the national Children's Research Centre (CRC, 2013), where the aim is to empower children and young people to undertake their own research investigations on subjects that are important to them. Children themselves have conducted numerous research studies for the CRC on a range of topics, including children's views on education, internet safety and young people's political views.

Clark and Moss's (2005) MOSAIC method, and the later adapted multi-modal map-making technique (Clark, 2011), both represent creative approaches designed specifically to engage with very young children (five years and under). The MOSAIC method involved different creative techniques such as book-making, the use of photography and drawing, map-making and also interviews with children in order to gain insight into the perspectives of very young children, and playing to their 'strengths' by '[broadening] the range of modes of expression which are given status within the research' (Clark, 2011, p 313). Clark developed this method further in her map-making project with young children, in which the children themselves used their own photographs in order to 'build up a map of their immediate environment – their nursery, school or play area' (Clark, 2011, p 315). The resulting creative data was then used in discussions with architects about school and nursery design issues with the aim of trying to ensure future building projects were designed with children's perspectives in mind.

Both Clark's and Clark and Moss's research draws on ethnographic and participant observation methods, and in Clark's mapping research specifically, suggests a close association between ethnographic and participatory approaches (see, for example, Clark, 2011). While it is clear that the methods used in these projects (as well as other creative methods with children) successfully engage with children in more direct and inclusive ways, as well as in ways that emphasise their creative 'voices' in research, the participatory element/s involved are simply referred to as ways of demonstrating 'children's agency in this process', which, in the main, is achieved through giving children opportunities to contribute meaning-making as well as to the production of knowledge. However, these are not necessarily, and arguably should not be, the only objectives or principles that distinguish participatory approaches in PR. Furthermore, the particular nature and extent of children's agentic involvement and its association with a clear participatory approach (with respect to children's active involvement in research, their degree of autonomy and understanding about participation, their capacity to act as co-researchers and for the research to bring about social change) is not always made clear in these and other types of projects that claim to be participatory in both principle and design. This is not to suggest any shortcomings on the part of these kinds of research studies, the methods developed or the intentions of the researchers themselves.[5] Rather, what would be helpful for researchers who are wrestling with some of these participatory and methodological issues is clearer reference to more coherent participatory frameworks or models of working, so that researchers are able to locate their research projects and methods at a point or place on or within such a framework (see, for example, Chapter Six, Figure 6.1), and with reference to clear directives in terms of broader social and political outcomes.[6]

While it is clear that some children choose to participate (or not) in research depending on a number of factors, including the perceived benefits to them of taking part, the degree of intrusion involved, whether they consider the rewards worth it (whether personal or altruistic), and whether they have the time or inclination to participate (see Kirby and Bryson, 2002; Hill, 2006), children's decisions will also inevitably be influenced by the degree to which researchers engage and work ethically with children, as has been stated. They will also be determined by the degree of expertise researchers possess in working effectively with children, the extent to which research is genuinely participatory (as opposed to simply tokenistic; see Hart, 1992; see also Chapter Six, Figure 6.1), *and* where there is recognition *both* that children 'are permanently a part of social renewal, and from an early age are an integral part of social organisation' (Qvortrup, 1985, p 142), but, like other vulnerable or marginalised groups, may also be 'in need of special, group-differentiated protections' (Stasiulis, 2002, p 507).

In addition, while it is obvious that not all children are part of a homogeneous group with the same opportunities, disadvantages or vulnerabilities, it is also the case that conducting research with distinct groups or 'communities' of children and young people is not always possible because of the nature and extent of their marginalisation or vulnerability. Thus, while numerous childhood research studies have been conducted at a collective or 'community' level – research on school children, for example (Clark and Moss, 2005; Madge et al, 2012), and those taking part in community youth projects (Kelly, 2011) – some children are much more difficult to identify and access as part of a recognised group, sub-group or community. This is particularly the case for multiply vulnerable children, such as those who have experienced abuse, neglect or trauma, those who live in families affected by substance misuse, mental illness and so on, and for many of these children choosing not to disclose these problems or circumstances may be deliberate in order to avoid further harm or neglect, or risk or safeguarding assessments that might lead to family separations. This has been particularly true for children identified as young carers who, before their needs were recognised in research, policy and practice in the UK, were reluctant to come forward for help and support as a consequence of these fears.

It is to this group of vulnerable children I now turn as a way of demonstrating directly through research practice (and the underpinning conceptual and theoretical paradigms relating to children's rights and the 'new' sociology of childhood) how PR approaches are relevant to, and have been introduced within, young carers' research. Using the particular example of research on young carers (and their families) thus demonstrates:

- The social and political transformations that have occurred as a result of research strategies that have facilitated and enhanced the voices of young carers in research – how children themselves (as carers) have been included in research, policy and practice as a result of approaches that engage directly with children themselves.
- The need for a sound theoretical and conceptual framework to underpin (participatory) research strategies.
- How PR approaches develop and can be informed by children themselves (and with reference to relevant ethical frameworks and guidance).
- How participatory approaches with young carers (and other vulnerable groups) can and have evolved, and can also be conducted at the inclusive and 'emancipatory' levels in PR (see Chapter Six, Figure 6.1).

Research with young carers (and their families)

> [Young carers' research] together with the growing body of sociological and social policy research which attempts to listen to the voices of children in poverty is underpinned by a recognition of children's agency – in other words that they are social actors who, to quote Gerry Redmond often exercise "creativity … in coping with their situation, and in improving their own lives, and those of their families" and are not simply passive objects of decisions made by their parents or professionals. (Lister, 2013)

Research on young carers[7] started in the UK in the early 1990s with a small-scale research study into the experiences and needs of just 14 young carers (see Aldridge and Becker, 1993). Prior to this time, young carers had not been recognised in public or political discourses or in health and social care policy and practice, which had focused entirely on the experiences and needs of adult carers until this time. However, messages from health and social work practice, for example, had begun to show that children were undertaking informal caring responsibilities in families affected by parental illness or disability, especially in the absence of other forms of (informal and formal) support. Because children had not been recognised as contributing to informal care in families affected by parental illness or disability prior to this time – and were thus hidden, marginalised or considered 'hard to reach' – conducting research in this field meant that initial investigations inevitably had to adopt small-scale, qualitative approaches rather than (large-scale) quantitative methods. Thus, while it was acknowledged that in order to ensure these children were supported appropriately, numbers or statistics would at some point be needed that would show the *extent* of the problem (providing estimates about the numbers of children engaged in informal care provision in domestic settings), and it was necessary to raise awareness of the issue by first gaining insight into the *nature* of children's caring experiences. At the same time, it was always understood that their status both as children *and* as 'hidden' (informal) carers living in families affected by parental illness or disability meant that these children were multiply vulnerable and would thus require research methods that would be sensitive to this fact. In which case, talking directly with children about their caring experiences using in-depth qualitative methods was considered to be the most appropriate and sensitive way of conducting research with them and their families at this early stage of research development.

Notably, although evidence from the numerous subsequent studies of young carers conducted in the mid to late 1990s resulted in the recognition of their *collective* needs (that is, as a sub-group of vulnerable children), the early small-scale investigations involved talking to *individual* children (and their families; see Aldridge and Becker, 1993, 1994), the majority of whom were not recognised or included in health or social care policy or practice, and who were also marginalised, isolated or 'hidden' with no connection to any known group or sub-group of vulnerable children, agency or support service at that time. Indeed, this fact alone meant that identifying and gaining access to children to take part in the research in the first place proved a considerable challenge and was made possible only through established networks and contacts with individual health and social care professionals who were aware of families where parents had chronic illness or disability, and who were having to rely on their children for care.[8] Thus, the phase prior to fieldwork taking place proved to be a critical, albeit lengthy, preparatory process involving careful negotiations with known health and social care professionals (for example, GPs, hospital consultants, social workers, health visitors, and so on) who knew of relevant families, and who were willing to act as intermediaries by talking to parents and children about their possible participation in the study.

It is important to point out that while the intention at this time was not purposefully to adopt a participatory approach, or certainly not as we may understand PR today, nevertheless, the objective was to talk directly to children themselves and to ask them about their experiences of living with and caring for a parent (or other relative in the home) who was chronically sick or had a disability. This was the first time research on this topic had been attempted, and these kinds of methods, that relied on building rapport and trusting relationships with professionals and children and families alike, were less commonly used at that time when researching the impacts of chronic illness or disability on family life.[9]

Although two small-scale social research studies in the late 1980s had revealed evidence of young caring in families, the methods used in these projects relied entirely on second-hand or anecdotal accounts from others such as adults or teachers, and not on evidence from the children themselves (see O'Neill, 1988; Page, 1988). Furthermore, children's caring responsibilities had been identified as one of the (numerous) outcomes of parental illness or disability in families prior to this time (see Sturges, 1978), but the consequences for children here were described very much in negative terms, psychologically, emotionally, and in terms of children's so-called 'abnormal' socialisation and development (see also Anthony, 1970). In fact, the more pernicious consequences of this evidence for children and families is perhaps reflected in the fear they had of disclosing children's caring responsibilities in families affected by parental illness or disability, and that this may lead to family separations. The methods used and conclusions drawn in these medical studies relied very much on clinical (laboratory-based) observations and assumptions about the impacts of parental 'disorders' on children and family life more generally. An example here is Anthony's medical research into the impact on families of physical and mental illness among parents, which he described as a crisis for the whole family that would only be resolved on the death of the parent, or where families survived these 'crises' through self-reliance. As a result of his clinical observations in this field, Anthony concluded (1970, p 62):

> We therefore find families that are disorganised, suspicious, chaotic and fluctuating ... within the interpersonal matrix, a great deal of psychopathology can develop insidiously within individuals, *especially children*, without its becoming recognisable. Abnormal attitudes and behaviour are assimilated and symptoms are enhanced with sometimes extraordinary facility. In this sort of setting, some small psychological epidemics frequently occur. (emphasis added)

Less than three decades later, research into the impact of parental illness or disability on children intended to gain more holistic insights by investigating the outcomes for children in terms of their own health *and* social care needs by talking directly to children and young people themselves (see Bilsborrow, 1992; Becker et al, 1998). While the methods used in many of these studies may not have been purposefully aligned with a distinct participatory approach, as has been stated, the underlying intention was indeed sympathetic to an inclusive or participatory philosophy or ideal that, for the first time, gave children and young people – in this case, young carers – a voice.[10]

The voices of young carers in research

The two early studies with young carers and their families used in-depth interviews with just 14 children (Aldridge and Becker, 1993) and subsequently their parents (Aldridge and Becker, 1994). Both studies used semi-structured questions to elicit qualitative data relating to the nature and extent of children's caring responsibilities and the impact of caring on their lives. The follow-up study in 1994 asked parents – who were (differently) vulnerable because of the nature of their illness/disability – their views about their experiences of having to rely on informal care and support from their children. At the time of the first study in 1993, it was evident that both children and parents were concerned about the impact of disclosing children's caring activities in the home for fear that risk assessments would be implemented that would result in family separations (see also Meredith, 1991). However, what was also clear from talking to the children who participated in the study was that they were undertaking the kind of (unsupported) caring responsibilities that we would usually associate with adulthood:

> To help my dad out I dress him, take him to the toilet, keep him warm, listen for him in the night, give him medicines, watch him because when he smokes he drops his fags on the floor, he might set light to himself. (Jas, quoted in Aldridge and Becker, 1993, p 19)

Taken collectively, the children's accounts presented a picture of the nature and extent of their informal caring activities and responsibilities that had not been revealed before. Evidence from these early studies showed that children were providing a range of practical and emotional support for parents (or other relatives in the home) who were ill or who had a disability, including housework (cooking, cleaning), managing budgets and finances, caring for or 'babysitting' siblings, lifting or helping with mobility for parents who had injuries or physical disabilities as well as undertaking intimate and nursing-type responsibilities (including administering medication, bathing and toileting parents). Subsequent studies also revealed the extent of children's emotional support (such as 'being with' parents when they were down, talking to them, reassuring them), especially in families where parents had mental health problems such as depression or anxiety disorders (see Aldridge and Becker, 2003; see also Becker et al, 1998; Göpfert et al, 1999).

The stories of the children and young people who took part in these studies – used verbatim in the 1993 study and in subsequent investigations – served two important purposes. First, they showed the nature, extent and impact of children's caring responsibilities that were disproportionate to their age and level of maturity (described at the time as the 'unacceptable face of community care'; see Meredith, 1991); and second, for the first time ever they gave young carers a voice that proved to be a powerful catalyst for change. The following extract, from the 1993 study, of 16-year-old Jimmy's account of caring for his terminally ill father (who had died just prior to the interview with Jimmy himself) illustrates clearly, and powerfully, these aspects of the research:

> When I think about all those years I cared for my dad, it makes me angry, not because I had to care for him – I wanted to care for him – but because I was left alone to cope with his illness for so long. I wasn't just doing ordinary tasks like other kids might do around the house. I was having to cook for him ... take him to the toilet, clean him up when he couldn't get to the toilet – because he couldn't get up the stairs towards the end. No one should have to see their parents like that, when they lose all their bodily functions. I loved my dad and I couldn't bear to see him losing his dignity – getting more ill before my eyes. (quoted in Aldridge and Becker, 1993, p vi)

This methodological approach, using in-depth interviews and research 'conversations' that utilised and promoted the voices of young carers themselves, in research reports and other outputs from these studies, also proved to be an effective way of working practically with children in research. The method relied on building rapport and relationships of trust and confidentiality with children and their families which were critical stages in the preparatory work prior to the data collection phase, and resulted in greater understanding and mutuality in researcher–participant relationships. However, as has been stated, it cannot be claimed that the research aligned itself specifically to distinct PR methodological and epistemological frameworks or paradigms because ideas about new ways of involving children (and other vulnerable groups) in research were evolving at that time and were far from fully developed. Neither were the methods used in the early studies with young carers congruent with the types of methods that might be used today at the 'top-end', or 'emancipatory' level in PR, or where children are involved 'in all aspects of the research in a meaningful way, from the beginning through to the end' (NCAS, 2013, p 4).

Nevertheless, both philosophically and in intention, this research was informed and underpinned by recognition of children's rights (to participate, to have a voice) and an ethical approach that involved dialogue with the children themselves as part of an ongoing or continuous process. Thus, the methods used were designed on the basis of generating data that were based on what *children themselves said*, rather than on second-hand accounts from their parents or what adult professionals said about them and their needs (see also Lister, 2013). Furthermore, the analysis, discussion and recommendations from these research studies were informed entirely by the experiences and narratives of the children themselves (and those of parents and professionals in subsequent studies). Thus, in the early studies, the thematic analysis of the interview data, while not conducted collaboratively with the children themselves (as might be the case in PR that locates itself higher on the participatory scale, or Participatory Model – see Chapter Six, Figure 6.1), neither was it based on any specific or pre-ordained hypothesis. This was genuinely uncharted research territory investigating an entirely new social issue or phenomenon. The verbatim quotes were not 'cherry-picked' (see Richardson, 1994) in order to fit or complement some established hypothesis, but were used to illustrate themes that had been identified based entirely on the interview data with the children themselves.

Thus, the recommendations from this research were also based on what the children themselves had said they needed most, including practical support from health, social care and education services; information about illnesses or disabilities, provided and written in ways that children could understand; recognition that they wanted to be able to choose whether they provided help or support to parents; and 'someone to talk to' about their experiences and needs (see Aldridge and Becker, 1993, p 66). The implications both of the findings from the study and the recommendations they generated were also discussed in further outputs from the study that proposed the types of health and social care services that were needed to support young carers and their families, as well as the policy implications.[11]

This approach was also critical in recognising young carers' multiply vulnerable status both innately and circumstantially – as children *and* as carers – and in terms of research governance and ethical perspectives (see the discussion above). The approach was also significant not just in ensuring the narratives and voices of young carers were heard in public and political arenas, but also in informing further research strategies and dialogues about children's resilience (see Aldridge and Wates, 2004; Aldridge and Sharpe, 2007; Skovdal et al, 2009), as well as contributing to methods discourses about children's vulnerability and participation (see Aldridge, 2012a; Graham et al, 2013). It was also recognised in subsequent studies on young caring that as well as the need for qualitative data about young carers' experiences of care, quantitative data that focused on the prevalence and incidence of young caring in the UK were also required. Thus, further studies used in-depth interview and focus group methods as well as surveys and methods that combined these different approaches (see also Dearden and Becker, 1995, 1998). Furthermore, the relevance of a rights-based agenda and framework for developing and advancing research, policy and practice on young carers (and their families) was made more concrete in a number of key publications that discussed children's rights more broadly at a national level (see Franklin, 2002), and this has culminated more recently in the inclusion of young carers' rights globally in the UN *Convention on the Rights of the Child*.

New directions for policy and practice

As discussed in Chapter One, guiding principles in PR should ensure that participatory studies are allied both conceptually and theoretically to relevant precepts and epistemologies *and* should provide clear directions for policy and practice. In many respects the programme of research on young caring fulfilled these objectives from the outset, even if 'emancipatory' PR approaches were developed later in the evolution of young carers' research. The programme of research on young carers has drawn on, and been informed by, 'new' sociological perspectives on childhood and the idea (and practice) of children's active contributions to research, policy and practice. As has been stated, it is also underpinned conceptually by a children's rights framework.

Evidence of the significance of the policy and practice directives resulting from this research is also clear in the numerous changes to health and social care policy and practice in the UK that have occurred since the mid-1990s, and that have been based on the data and recommendations from these studies. Following the Early Day Motion that was tabled based on the 1993 research (Aldridge and Becker, 1993), young carers were included in the Carers (Recognition and Services) Act 1995 and subsequently the National Carers Strategy 2008 and 2010, the Framework for the Assessment of Children in Need and their Families 2010, and the Carers and Disabled Children's Act 2000. Evidence from young carers' research has also been used in the 2008 House of Commons Select Committee on vulnerable children, as well as in the consultation process for the Coalition government's draft Care and Support Bill and Children and Families Bill.[12] These policy changes represent important outcomes for this and other kinds of research that adopt more inclusive, participatory approaches (see the discussion earlier in Chapter One) with vulnerable populations in that they demonstrate the efficacy and rigour of research that uses less conventional methods (alongside other more traditional methods) and that, importantly, also emphasise individuality, inclusivity and voice. The points below highlight the strategic ways in which policy and practice directives were incorporated into research processes and in outputs from the young carers' research:

- Based on research evidence provided by young carers (and their families), through their verbatim accounts and narratives, as well as subsequently through survey-based quantitative data and multi-method approaches, key recommendations were made for policy and practice regarding the needs and rights of young carers and their families in all outputs from the research.
- Strategies for translating evidence into policy and practice relied on a multi-phased approach that meant communicating messages from the research (based on what young carers themselves had said) to health, social care and education professionals (through published articles in professional journals, presentations at conferences, seminars and communication through known networks and organisations), media professionals (editors, journalists), policy makers and key stakeholders (MPs, directors of social services, children's services, and so on), as well as via the academic community (through published articles in academic journals, books, book chapters, and so on).
- Communicating with research participants throughout the phases of research was critical – in initial relationship-building phases prior to fieldwork taking place, through the data collection phase and at the outputs stage when key messages and recommendations from the research were reported back to young carers and their families.

- Emphasising and promoting young carers' participation and voices in research has been critical throughout the programme of research with young carers and their families, including in later and ongoing research where young carers have been engaged in collaborative ways (see below), and have also been invited to participate in conferences and seminars and to report and present findings themselves to key stakeholders, professionals and policy makers.[13]

Such strategies have enabled the continuation and advancement of research in this field, and have ensured that evidence is used not only to inform and shape policy and practice, but also to transform lives. As a direct result of the programme of research on young carers conducted by the Young Carers Research Group and others (see Bilsborrow, 1992; Mahon and Higgins, 1995), numerous statutory and voluntary sector services have been introduced that provide dedicated services to young carers and their families (for example, young carers projects – there are now more than 130 such projects across the UK), as well as provide support to ill or disabled adults in their parenting roles. Thus, the programme of research on young caring has led to important and necessary policy and practice changes that have helped improve the lives of young carers and their families.

Developing and advancing participatory research methods with young carers

A turning point in the programme of research on young carers and their families in PR terms specifically came in the 2001 study of the experiences and needs of children who lived with and cared for parents who had serious and enduring mental health problems (Aldridge and Becker, 2003). This two-year study took a triangulated approach (see also Clark and Moss, 2001) by working closely with children (who were caring for their parents with mental illness), their parents, and the professionals who were providing formal support services to families. The intention was to use two-phase, in-depth interviews with both children and their parents who were on the Care Programme Approach (Enhanced Level). From a research governance and ethical perspective this involved working with multiply vulnerable children *and* their parents. In total, 40 children and their parents took part in the study, as well as a range of professionals involved in providing formal care services to families. Data from the study were significant in contributing new knowledge about children's experiences of living with and caring for parents with mental health problems as well as in addressing, and also refuting, to some extent, risk or harm assumptions that, from a health and social care perspective, suggested children were *inevitably* at increased risk of harm or development delay as a direct result of parental mental illness in families (see Aldridge and Becker, 2003). Positive aspects of parent–child relationships were also revealed in the findings from the study, as well as the impact on these relationships of sudden downturns in parents' mental health – as illustrated in the following example from one of the children who took part in the study, who was caring for her mother who had bipolar disorder:

> She is just so funny, you know, when she's well, she is just the best mum ever. She's just funny and everything, you now, has a laugh with you. She's not like a normal mum, you can tell her about anything, you know, boys or anything like that ... she'll understand.... And then when she's not well, then, we still get on with her, because even though she's nasty to us, I haven't got the heart to be nasty to her back. Because I still love her and it's not her fault. (Julia, 15, quoted in Aldridge and Becker, 2003, p 85)

While this remains the first study of its kind to take this three-way perspective, and has also contributed to the development and advancement of social and family models of mental illness (see Falkov, 2013) that focus on the experiences and needs of families rather than just adult patients (the medical model), a number of methodological and ethical challenges were also encountered that pointed to the need for different kinds of participatory methods in order to work more inclusively with children and young people (see Aldridge, 2013). In this sense, the mental health study served as a catalyst for developing new methodological approaches with multiply vulnerable young carers.

Identifying and accessing participants for the study was a lengthy process that relied on collaboration with key professionals and stakeholders who were willing to mediate and ask families with whom they were in contact if they would be willing to take part in the research (these 'mediators' included young carers' project staff who offered dedicated services to young carers and their families, and also Rethink staff who were the research partners on the project).

While the project was conducted in accordance with recognised ethical guidelines – specifically, issues of consent, permission, confidentiality and so on were managed at both a local (institutional) and national level (with reference to Department of Health and British Psychological Society guidance) and in recognition of the needs of vulnerable groups[14] – it was in the process of working with both children and parents on the project that the key challenges lay, particularly because their lives were often difficult and subject to rapid change. This was evidenced in the fact that, depending on parents' state of health at the time, their ability and willingness to participate in the interviews varied considerably, which also had an impact on their children's availability to take part. Furthermore, during the course of the fieldwork some parents were hospitalised either voluntarily or sectioned under the Mental Health Act 1983. In some cases children didn't even know this and had returned home from school to an empty house (lack of communication from adult mental health service professionals with children's services as well as with children themselves were key findings from the study; see Aldridge and Becker, 2003). Thus, for many children in the study (and indeed, for families as a whole) their lives were in constant transition and flux, and were also difficult emotionally as well as practically, and all of these issues had an impact (to a lesser or greater degree) on their ability and willingness to participate in the study.

The mental health study therefore revealed particular challenges in engaging with children and young people, and adults (parents who were mentally ill) who experienced multiple vulnerabilities. It was also clear from this study that some children simply do not want to talk about their experiences or may feel unable to articulate their views through methods that rely on their verbal contributions. In terms of conducting fieldwork with participants such as these, despite the skills and expertise of researchers in working with vulnerable or marginalised people, it can still be the case that interviews need to be abandoned because participants, having agreed to participate in principle, do not wish to take part when the time comes for the interview itself to take place. This is illustrated in an example from the study in which a 13-year-old boy (who cared for his mother who had bipolar disorder) agreed to the interview taking place at his house at a given time, but who simply would not talk to the researcher when they arrived to conduct the interview. In many respects this is understandable, and especially given the context of this particular study – very few of the children who took part had been given the opportunity to talk about their experiences or needs to anyone else outside the immediate family – and it was also clear that many of the children (and parents) were fearful that disclosures of caring might lead to family separations.

Thus, even qualitative methods that rely on eliciting individual stories or narratives through interviews or research 'conversations' may not always be the best way of obtaining data from differently vulnerable participants (those who don't want or feel unable to verbalise their experiences in ways that they might wish or that fit with research objectives using conventional qualitative methods). However, one of the obvious concerns when participants are unwilling or unable to verbalise their experiences and needs in these ways – in qualitative studies that use conventional interview or focus group techniques, for example – is that it becomes much more likely that they will be excluded from these studies if they present as reluctant or challenging in research design and recruitment terms, and this can only serve to further marginalise or exclude already vulnerable individuals and groups. Participatory approaches that are designed specifically with the needs of vulnerable participants in mind, and in consultation with them, are thus perhaps more likely to capture insights into their experiences that may have remained hidden for some time. They are also more likely to fulfil the needs of participants who are reluctant to be just the objects/subjects of study or, even in studies that use tried and tested qualitative methods, are unwilling or unable to take part in ways that rely only on their verbal contributions.

'Pictures of young caring': photographic participation and elicitation research

Evidence from studies within visual sociology, and from research in other disciplines and fields, suggest that participatory visual methods can help overcome problems some participants may encounter when asked to recall and recount their experiences verbally (see also the discussion later in Chapter Three). Evidence from photographic studies suggests that these methods may be particularly useful when working with vulnerable individuals or groups (see Greek, 2005; Campbell and O'Neill, 2006; Thomson, 2008; Joanou, 2009; Catalani and Minkler, 2010). Some commentators have proposed that visual methods such as PhotoVoice or photo diaries can provide insight into unseen or hard-to-reach locations and 'hidden' experiences, and that they can help to 'bridge the gaps between researcher and researched' (Joanou, 2009, p 214). Pillow also emphasises the reciprocity in photographic methods that help to '[equalise] research relationships' (2003, p 179). Even among very young children, photographic methods can contribute to 'meaning-making' and 'cultural brokerage', especially when other creative methods are used alongside photographic techniques, an example here being Clark and Moss's (2005) MOSAIC approach and Clark's (2011) multi-modal mapping methods, as already discussed.

With respect to research with vulnerable children and young people specifically, it is argued that the use of photographic methods can also help challenge fixed perceptions and assumptions about children's lack of competency or agency, and can help children themselves to gain a sense of control in research processes. In her discussion about using visual research methods with children and young people, for example, Thomson (2008, p 5) argues that their 'critical voice' is essential in ensuring that, as speakers they exercise 'some agency and control of circumstances which previously felt beyond their reach.' This was certainly the case when using photographic participation and elicitation methods with young carers.

One of the main objectives of the participatory photographic study was to ensure children who didn't want to participate in interview-based research about their experiences of living with and caring for parents who had serious mental health problems could participate using methods that did not rely on their verbal contributions. Further methodological and epistemological objectives were to measure and understand the usefulness of the method from the perspectives of the children themselves, and to gain greater insight into the needs and resilience of young carers.

Sixteen young carers took part in the study, each of whom was caring for a parent who had serious and enduring mental health problems. The young carers compiled photographic diaries using disposable cameras, and were asked to record aspects of their lives that were meaningful to them as carers over a period of two weeks. In this way they were able to exercise a degree of control and agency over what they wanted to photograph, and thus the content of the data they contributed to the study, as well as when and where data collection took place. Boddy and Smith (2008, p 63) have argued that diary compilation research methods such as these can provide opportunities for participants to record 'everyday life' events that have meaning for them as well as generate data that is both rich in content and methodologically robust. A total of 287 photographs were taken by the children and young people, and both content and thematic analyses were conducted on the images, hard copies of which were also used as part of the elicitation phase of the study as prompts (see also Collier and Collier, 1986) to help generate discussions about the photographs (and their 'meanings'), but only if the children chose to participate in this phase of the project. Thus, the children themselves played an integral part in the analytical phase of the research by providing thematic (and meaningful) context to their visual narratives or stories.

The content analysis was made up of two distinct phases that focused on 'internal' and 'external' narratives derived from the photographic data, and was also informed by the children's own analyses. Banks (2001, p 11) defines the internal narrative as 'the story, if you will, that the image communicates', and the external narrative as 'the social context that produced the image, and the social relations within which the image is embedded at any moment of viewing.' The children's photographs (without any accompanying narrative or text) were made available as personalised photographic 'albums' on the Young Carers Research Group website (www.ycrg.org.uk). These collections demonstrate important aspects of the participatory approach – they confer 'ownership' of the images on the children who participated in the study, and at the same time are indicative of their involvement in decisions about how these images were represented publicly. The children were keen for the photographs to be presented as they were, to 'tell their own story' without accompanying textual narratives – in this sense, the researcher and the research group also took on the role of 'banker, retaining data/information ... but giving others access to it' (Lewis and Porter, 2004 p 194). In the final report and other outputs from the study, the images reveal specific aspects of caring through the combination of the visual and textual. Given that some of the children wanted to 'explain' or 'tell' their visual stories (using the photographs as visual prompts), some of the images are presented with the children's accompanying written accounts, and these represent a very personalised visual-textual discourse on children's caring experiences and their relationships with their parents, as demonstrated in the following examples:

Photograph 1: 'Parents'

That's a picture of my mum and dad; you just want to hug them. I'm a carer for my mum. On a really, really, really, bad day I will be doing absolutely nearly everything. Dressing her, doing washing, vacuuming, cleaning, and loads of things. These two weeks why I did not show anything in these photos is because these two weeks were perfect, they've been very good. What dad does is try and get money so he comes up with some weird and wonderful things, and he's trying to get on the market. He's always trying to do something new. He's trying to just get some money in. (Fiona, 13, quoted in Aldridge and Sharpe, 2007, p 11)

Photographs 2, 'Keys' **and 3,** 'Medication'

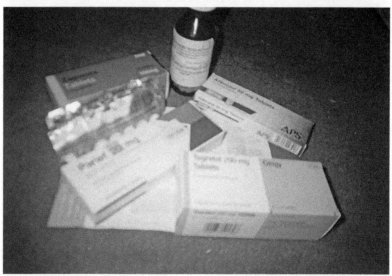

When my mum is ill I have to lock all the doors and we are not allowed to answer the phone because she thinks somebody is going to hurt us and stuff. It used to make me feel unhappy but not anymore. I'm supporting mum. Sometimes I do get a bit annoyed. The next one is a prescription I go down and get for my mother. I know what the medication does but I'm not sure which one does which. It says it all on the medication. When I follow her to the doctors I wait in the waiting room. I take her but then she has to go in by herself because she goes in and talks and does not want to upset me. I check her medication when she's got home or when she's feeling ill and times like that I have to go and get them personally and make sure she takes them and watch her. (Emma, 14, quoted in Aldridge and Sharpe, 2007, p 13)

The intention from the outset of the photographic study with young carers was to find ways of including (multiply vulnerable) children and young people in research processes that did not rely solely on their verbal contributions, and that would allow them opportunities to express themselves in other ways. Thomson argues that when children have been involved in producing visual data they should also be involved in selection and editing processes, 'so that their assumptions are also made explicit and available for discussion' (2008, p 9). What was interesting in the Pictures of Young Caring study was that in all cases the children wanted to participate in the selection process, and their involvement during the analytical phase was clearly very important to them. Most of the children also chose to participate in the elicitation phase of the study by using the photographs they had taken themselves as prompts in telling their visual stories. Not all of the children wanted each of their photographs to be presented with accompanying narratives when these were included in the final report and other outputs. Without exception, all of the children were positive about the photographic method and its usefulness in terms of presenting opportunities to participate in research in different (visual rather than verbal) ways. The practical success of this method in engaging children in more inclusive ways via techniques that they can enjoy (as opposed, perhaps, simply to endure) is demonstrated in the fact that a number of young carers' projects in the UK are now using photographic workshops and other visual methods as a way of engaging and communicating with children who are new to projects or who are reluctant to 'open up' in one-to-one or group discussions.

These methods are also being considered in other settings, for example, in primary health care consultations with children and young people (see Aldridge, 2010).

Children's participation and social change outcomes

The photographic study involving young carers is just one example of the different types of creative, sensory methods available to researchers when planning participatory projects with children and young people (including multiply vulnerable or marginalised children). The intention in outlining both the photographic method and the project itself was not to describe or discuss the findings from the study in detail, as these are available elsewhere (see Aldridge and Sharpe, 2007). Rather, the intention was to demonstrate both the potential and value of these kinds of PR techniques when working more collaboratively with children (these methods are also discussed in more detail in the following chapter with respect to visual methods with people with profound learning difficulties). However, a further issue for consideration when using these kinds of methods is the challenge of using such PR methods with children – that emphasise collaboration and 'voice' – in broader social and political contexts where the participation rights of children are not always recognised or acted on.

Thus, while it is important to recognise children's roles in research, for example, as collaborators, as research actors, and so on, these shifts in thinking about children's participation also need to be reflected in broader contexts and in other areas of children's lived lives. Arguably, without such parity, the opportunities for PR with children to influence important and necessary social change outcomes are considerably reduced. Furthermore, such a shift in thinking about children's roles and contributions – as well as the phase of childhood itself – outside research environs will no doubt be slower to manifest in certain settings and will also require research evidence, researchers and children alike to reinforce the message that children are more than simply non-adult subjects, and it is here where research relationships are also critical. This would also seem to suggest that PR with children that is located at the 'top end' or 'emancipatory' level (see Chapter Six), while laudable in so many respects, may also remain simply aspirational as long as there is a lack of parity between the ways in which children's roles and contributions are perceived in different areas of their lives.

In one sense, direct evidence of this lack of equivalence was clear in the output phase of the photographic study with young carers. One of the important aims of the participatory project was to move beyond research that treats children simply as the objects of, or even the subjects in, research, but to consider them as collaborators or co-researchers, including in the outputs phase, by encouraging their input in helping to translate messages from the research in public arenas and discourses. Thus, all of the children and young people who participated in the study had been invited to take part in media work that would enable them to show their photographic work and skills, as well as convey important messages about what it was like for them living with and caring for parents who had mental health problems (and thus also helping to challenge stereotypes and misconceptions about mental illness in families). However, it was clear from the children's experiences of this process that media professionals – particularly in the print media – were not interested in publicising findings from the study in which the children were presented as photographers in the research project or as visual chroniclers of their own lives and experiences; rather, they presented the photographs of young caring as if these images had been taken by news photographers themselves, and used these images to support the textual narrative or story of 'suffering' young carers (see, for example, *The Observer*, 2008).

Despite the participatory objectives of the research project itself and the social change intentions that were underpinned empirically by an emphasis on children's direct involvement in the research (as photographers, as co-researchers), in media discourses particularly, their voices were silenced through media practices that failed entirely to acknowledge the children's contributions. Thus, despite the best (participatory) intentions of the research project, the children themselves, as co-researchers, were not able to influence or control entirely the ways in which the research findings (the photographic data) were interpreted and re-presented in other settings and by different third parties (in this case by individual media practitioners).

This example suggests a number of important issues for consideration:

- The role of the researcher as advocate, supporter and *co*-researcher throughout the research process is vital, and suggests genuinely emancipatory-level research (giving control to children at *all* stages of the research process) is not always achievable.
- Emancipatory, top-end PR objectives and principles can be compromised by other, external factors and influences that may be entirely out of the control of both participant and researcher.
- Children's dual status in society – as children at risk and as children with citizenship and participation rights – can also compromise,

or, at the very least, complicate, children's autonomy and ability to participate in PR that promotes emancipation.

Considered in these ways, both PR and PAR can be seen to have more limited outcomes or effects in terms of transforming children's lives as well as in influencing perceptions and constructions of childhood as a life phase. Put another way, the efficacy of children's voices in PR will only ever be as influential as the context in which these voices are heard and the ways in which children are perceived and treated. Of course, some argue that we should not confer adult or adult-type status on children because they need time and space to be children, but others would argue that at least they should be given choice in these matters – recognising their rights as individuals to choose and to contribute in whatever ways they would wish, and for many children this simply isn't the case.

Conclusion

> Only if genuine dialogue occurs between children and the adults in power will policies directed at social inclusion respond to children's felt needs, rather than to needs attributed to them. (Hill et al, 2004, p 80)

It is vital that children's voices are heard in research if their needs and rights are to be recognised and met in both policy and practice terms. However, as has been shown, a number of challenges and dilemmas arise when working with vulnerable children and young people in research, and particularly when attempting to work with them in more collaborative ways. Not least of these are the numerous, and often complex, ethical issues which must be managed and negotiated by researchers at the interface between participants, the institution (the academy) and regulation. In practice, this entails communication about, and implementation of, ethical procedures with children themselves and their parents (including obtaining permission, consent and ensuring confidentiality), and ensuring these procedures are congruent with, and meet the requirements of, ethics committees at a local, institutional level (university ethics committees, for example) as well as at a national level where necessary. Researchers must therefore work with the principles of research ethics conceptually, practically and personally (in research practice and in direct communications and relationships with participants, funders, and so on), as well as in more abstract terms (morally, philosophically, and so on).

As has already been shown, however, children and young people represent an obvious duality with respect to their *status* as children with distinct needs (for protection, for example), but also as *social agents* who demonstrate autonomy and competency in many different areas of their lives. This duality, and the tensions between different constructs and perceptions of childhood, have been addressed in research in a number of ways, including an increasing focus on children's inclusion, participation and voices both methodologically and in research praxis (working directly rather than abstractly or anecdotally with children); recognising the rights of children to choose whether to participate in research (as well as their right to refuse, or withdraw from, participation); asking children their views about the processes and outcomes (for them) of their participation in research (and in practice; see Kirby and Bryson, 2002; Hill, 2006), incorporating reflexive processes into research praxis that contribute new knowledge and understanding about children's needs and rights as participants in research and new ways of working collaboratively with them (see the discussion in Chapter Five); and the introduction of guidelines that acknowledge children's rights to participation and protection.[15]

Considering the example of research with young carers and their families, the fundamental aim of this work has been to ensure children's contributions to care are recognised (publicly and in policy and practice), and that such recognition is mirrored in both research methods and practice. A further intention has been to ensure that research processes themselves do not enhance children's vulnerability or compromise their identities or safety, and thus their rights (as children, as carers and as research participants) have been at the forefront of research planning and design. The research with young carers and their families described here represents a journey that is not simply a reflexive one, but one based on the practical development of different methods of incorporating, and enhancing, children's perspectives and voices in research.

As has been shown, numerous research studies have revealed the advantages of using creative methods in research, including participatory visual methods, with children and young people. However, in the absence of a clear and robust participatory framework, the link is not always made sufficiently clear in these studies between the methods used and the nature and extent of participation involved. Using less conventional creative participatory methodologies in research, including photographic participation techniques, also presents a number of unique challenges for the researcher when working with vulnerable or marginalised groups, and particularly in ethical terms, and it is to these issues that I turn in more detail in the following chapter when considering PR with people with learning difficulties.

THREE

Involving people with learning difficulties in participatory research

Introduction

Since the 1970s, disability research (as well as policy and practice) has been influenced by important theoretical and empirical advances in perspectives on, and understandings of, disability, evidenced specifically in the emergence of the social model of disability. This model proposes that disability is not a biological or medical human 'deficiency', but is influenced and shaped by social, political and economic factors, and is maintained through structural or systemic dynamics and ideologies. A number of important advances have also been made in the field of learning difficulty research,[1] although perhaps not to the same extent as in disability research more generally, as well as within the field of disability activism and the emergence of advocacy organisations and movements (for example, People First and the Norah Fry Research Centre), and in new government initiatives, policies and laws.[2] The inclusion of people with learning difficulties is now also a requirement of a number of funding agencies, 'as a condition of research funding' (Gilbert, 2004, p 298), and researchers with learning difficulties themselves have contributed their experiences, perspectives and expertise to learning difficulty research (see Atkinson and Williams, 1990; Aspis, 2000; Townson et al, 2004).

While these changes and new understandings have led to considerable improvements in the way learning difficulty is perceived, understood and managed, as well as to the empowerment of people with learning difficulties themselves, a number of challenges and tensions remain, particularly with respect to the social model and its relevance for people with learning difficulties, as well as in terms of research ethics and practice considerations. Furthermore, in order to prevent learning difficulty research becoming confined or restricted solely within its own field, or even in the broader arena of disabilities studies, some argue that it would be a positive step to see the inclusion of people with learning difficulties in general population studies using (tried and tested) participatory methods that are not incompatible with (or seen as barriers to) more conventional methods as part of a multi-method approach. These issues are explored in this chapter, drawing on relevant epistemological and methodological debates and evidence from research studies that use participatory methods with people with learning difficulties – and drawing on the specific examples of PR studies that use visual methods and PhotoVoice as part of multi-method projects (Booth and Booth, 2003; Sempik et al, 2005; Nind, 2008; Ollerton and Horsfall, 2013). The ethical challenges involved in working collaboratively with people with learning difficulties in PR, and particularly in studies that use visual methods, are also relevant to broader discourses about consent, privacy and confidentiality issues when using these kinds of approaches (and thus the discussion here also serves as an extension to the one introduced earlier in Chapter Two on this topic).

It is important to note that people with learning difficulties can encounter a number of unique challenges (including multiple impairments in some cases) that may result in their being defined or categorised in health and social care discourses, as well as in research governance and ethical terms, as multiply vulnerable. As such, supporting them through the delivery of health and social care services, in education and employment and in all other areas of their lives, will inevitably result in the focus of attention being on the nature (and extent) of these challenges and impairments. However, many of these difficulties also occur as a result of socially or structurally produced barriers to their full participation in society (and the social model of disability is relevant here – see the discussion below), and thus do not arise as a direct consequence of their learning difficulty alone. Thus, for the researcher working with people with learning difficulties (and indeed, any other multiply vulnerable group) it is critical that they are not seen *only* in these ways – simply as participants with learning difficulties. At the same time, it is also necessary to ensure that their individual needs, that occur as a result of their different abilities and experiences, are recognised and addressed through appropriate research methods and processes, and that additional barriers or challenges do not occur as a consequence of their participation in research.

Social model of disability and learning difficulty research

The social model has now become the ideological litmus test of disability politics in Britain used by the disabled people's movement to distinguish between organisations, policies, laws and ideas which are progressive, and those which are inadequate. (Shakespeare and Watson, 2001, p 9)

The social model of disability came about as a result of activism in the 1970s by members of the Union of the Physically Impaired Against Segregation (UPIAS), and was further developed by the work of a number of leading academics such as Finkelstein in the 1980s and Barnes and Oliver in the 1990s. Oliver's work (1990, 1997) is particularly significant with respect to his reference to personal tragedy theory that historically had seen people with learning difficulties (as well as other vulnerable groups such as those with physical and sensory impairments and mental illness) as needing help (and beneficence) coming to terms with their impairment, either through rehabilitation or removal from society. Despite the importance of the social model in recognising and resisting the oppression of people with disabilities by acknowledging the structural factors that reduced disability simply to a consequence of human deficiency, the experiences and needs of people with learning difficulties were, to a large extent, excluded from the social model paradigm until later in its evolution. Although, as Kiernan has noted (1999, p 45), this changed in the 1980s when people with learning difficulties began to be included as research participants, and their views were also sought with respect to evaluating the services they received, the impact of the social model on their lives was less notable, and specifically, as Chappell and colleagues argue, 'as an explicit framework for analysis' (2001, p 45). Indeed, at that time, these authors, and others like them, were calling for a more 'inclusive' social model that recognised and included the experiences and voices of people with learning difficulties, and thus moved away from the more narrow or exclusive focus on the needs of people with physical or sensory impairments. Indeed, others too have noted the relative exclusion of people with learning difficulties from social model discourse and analysis (see Kiernan, 1999; Gilbert, 2004).

Some of the explanations for this may lie to some extent in the epistemological tensions identified in subsequent critiques of the social model that pointed to problematic issues of (impairment/disability) dualism and identity within the social model (see Shakespeare and Watson, 2001; Goodley, 2013). With respect to the former, it was argued that the social model failed to acknowledge disability as impairment, as a form of bodily difference that can result in unique or inherent challenges and that have distinct physical consequences for those who experience impairments (such as pain, restriction of movement and so on; see Lewis and Porter, 2004; Emerson and Robertson, 2011). As Shakespeare and Watson (2001, p 9) have stated, 'we argue that the denial of difference is as big a problem for disability studies, as it was for feminism. Experientially, impairment is salient to many.... We are not just disabled people, we are also people with impairments, and to pretend otherwise is to ignore a major part of our biographies.'

In addition, the issue of identity (and identity politics) is also relevant, both in relation to the dialogue and debate that has occurred from within the field of critical disability studies regarding some of the problems or shortcomings of the social model, and with respect to the experiences and needs of people with learning difficulties themselves. Evidence from the self-advocacy movement shows that many people with learning difficulties do not necessarily relate to, or identify with, a disability identity, nor with perspectives that align learning difficulty with disability specifically (as discussed in Chapter One, the same is also true for people who are defined as 'vulnerable'). This is demonstrated in Goodley's (2000) self-advocacy research with people with learning difficulties. As one of the self-advocates stated, '"Learning disabilities" – I don't like that, disability makes you believe that we are in wheel chairs and we can't do anything for ourselves, when we can. We've got jobs now, we've got paid jobs' (quoted in Chappell and Goodley, 2001, p 46), self-advocate).

However, both self-identity and identity politics for people with learning difficulties are complex issues. While it is clearly important for many people with these kinds of challenges to distance themselves from the physical impairment or 'deficiency' associations with disability (as Dumbleton, 1998, has argued, the learning difficulty identity is significant in that it implies willingness and capacity to learn rather than a deficiency in learning), and this would seem to be congruent with the philosophy and principles enshrined within the social model paradigm, there are equal problems in denying impairments, particularly when they indicate or result in specific health or social care needs or the need for dedicated support (including support for independence or self-advocacy). These tensions or contrarieties can be explained (if not always resolved) by the complex and diverse ways in which learning difficulties manifest themselves in individuals as well as in the fact that people with learning difficulties are not part of a homogeneous group, but 'vary on every dimension' (Stalker, 1998, p 10), which, in many respects, is why participatory methods are necessary that are based on individualised accounts or case-by-case methods of data collection. They are also explained to some extent in the difference between intellectualising and action or between (social model) theory and practice. As Chappell and colleagues argue (2001, p 49), 'People with learning difficulties may be "doing" the social model, although not writing about it or articulating it in a theoretical language.'

Furthermore, it is perhaps when people experience severe, profound or multiple learning difficulties where questions about the relevance of the social model and the effects of dualism and identity politics (which, in many respects, are intellectually argued and analysed) are most pertinent. With respect to these issues, and particularly the social model's relevance to people with severe impairments or profound learning difficulties, French (1993, p 17) has argued, 'some of the most profound problems experienced by people with certain impairments are difficult, if not impossible, to solve by social manipulation.' However, it is vital that the particular challenges people with profound learning difficulties face are not perceived as problematic to the extent that their views on important aspects of their lives are overlooked – including the efficacy of health, social care and education services, for example – nor that they are considered too difficult to include in research studies that have direct relevance to their lives. Indeed, it is argued that both in terms of research methods and praxis, people with learning difficulties should be included in ways that 'capture *doing* as well as rhetoric' (Chappell et al, 2001, p 49, emphasis in original).

Participatory research with people with learning difficulties

The social model proposes different ways of seeing and constructing disability, based on what disabled people have said themselves about their experiences of disabling barriers in their lives, in which case, in empirical terms, this presupposes a participatory approach to research that emphasises inclusion and mutuality in research processes that enable the perspectives and experiences of disabled people and others with multiple impairments and difficulties to be heard. However, there are a number of problems with this supposition in practice. First, one of the proposed objectives of this kind of research that emphasises *doing* or action is that it should lead to transformation outcomes for the people involved (see Chapter One), as well as acknowledge and develop a framework for promoting 'the multiple constructions of reality' (Chevalier and Buckles, 2013, p 38). However, it is not always possible to plan, design or know in advance appropriate mechanisms for recognising and uncovering these multiple realities (and thus contribute to the development and advancement of theory and practice) when working with people with profound learning difficulties in research, even when using participatory approaches. Indeed, evidence suggests that qualitative research more generally with this group is relatively sparse, is often considered difficult, and has also diminished in certain fields over recent years (if measured by publications in health and education research, for example; see Porter and Lacey, 2005).

Second, there appears to be both a distinction – and at times some confusion or conflation – between 'emancipatory' research on the one hand, and participatory methods on the other, with respect to approaches adopted from a social model perspective and those from within the field of learning difficulty research. With respect to the former, 'emancipatory' approaches are underpinned by a commitment to social action and change outcomes that rely on participants taking control of research processes, as Gilbert (2004, p 300) outlines:

> In participatory approaches, the researcher works in partnership with participants, while the methods employed are qualitative with the aim of interpreting and explaining the experiences of people with learning disabilities. However, the researcher remains accountable to the funding body. In contrast, emancipatory approaches based on the social model of disability can employ either qualitative or quantitative methods in a research process where the researcher's expertise is placed at the disposal of people with disabilities. Emancipatory research is committed to changing the conditions of the relationship between the researcher and the researched.

We can see from this description that 'emancipatory' research based on the social model is closest to approaches aligned with or located at the top end of the Participatory Model (see Chapter Six, Figure 6.1), and is also most closely connected to the principles and objectives of PAR. However, leaving aside for the moment social model perspectives and intentions, in considering Gilbert's distinctions more carefully, it is not difficult to imagine how certain research methods and approaches may intersect or converge at a point somewhere between the participatory and 'emancipatory' modes (for example, accountability to funding bodies does not necessarily preclude emancipatory objectives or principles; or transformations may occur over time and even when research is predicated on accountability – to funders and so on). As discussed in Chapter One, in some respects it is perhaps more useful to consider PR and emancipatory objectives in research as part of a broader, more inclusive approach (see Walmsley and Johnson, 2003; see also Chapter One), but where it is necessary for researchers to locate their research objectives at a point on or within a relevant participatory framework (and to make this clear in their intentions, in their research proposals, designs, and so on) in order to avoid any ambiguities or potential for false claims about the research or expectations. In this way, PR, whether it is action-driven, based on 'emancipatory' principles, or in some cases, based on more realistic intentions that focus mainly on issues of power and mutuality in researcher–participant relationships (weighed against, for example, the demands of funding bodies, the academy etc; see Aldridge, 2012b), can also take into account inevitable tensions that arise between what is paragon and what is possible.

Practically speaking, however, while participatory approaches in learning difficulty research are considered both practicable and appropriate, they are also seen by some only as a 'step toward emancipatory research' (Kiernan, 1999, p 45). Notably, Kiernan further argues that in some cases it is difficult to see how people with learning difficulties can be involved at the emancipatory level, for example, in studies that focus on costs of community services or the 'challenging' behaviour of people with learning difficulties (in the same way that not all research about children can and should involve them directly – in certain studies of child abuse, for example). However, what was clear from debates in the 1990s about how and why people with learning difficulties had been largely excluded from research and service evaluations, as well as from social model theory and research, was the clear assumption in these debates that research methods, even in qualitative research studies, must rely on participants' verbal contributions – and the difficulties therein. There remained therefore somewhat fixed or conventional ideas, both about the nature of participation and the qualitative methodologies themselves.

An example here is Kiernan's observation that, 'in the end, people with severe learning disabilities and severe limitations in receptive and expressive communication will be unable to "participate" meaningfully despite further improvements in the *interview* skills of researchers. This seriously limits the scope of new paradigm research' (1999, p 46; emphasis added).

In his 2004 review of PR studies with people with learning difficulties, Gilbert also proposed that 'significant gaps remain in the way that research has so far been able to include people with learning disabilities. In no area are these gaps more apparent than with people with high support needs and severely impaired communication' (p 299), and Gilbert noted Atkinson's (1997) observation that people with severe or particular learning difficulties had formed alliances in research with non-learning disabled people because 'many have little or no access to either the *written or spoken word*' (Gilbert, 2004, p 300; emphasis added). The implication here is that people with learning difficulties are difficult to include in research at the emancipatory level, even in studies that use qualitative approaches that rely on, for example, interviewing, focus groups, research 'conversations', life history methodologies, and so on. However, as a number of commentators have argued, far from being indicative of the 'problem' that people with learning difficulties (or other disabilities, impairments or 'vulnerabilities') present in research, this is much more a reflection of the shortcomings of research methods themselves (see, for example, Booth, 1996; Goodley and Moore, 2000). Nevertheless, including people with *profound* learning difficulties and multiple impairments/vulnerabilities in research does present a number of methodological and ethical challenges, even in PR or inclusive research. In both epistemological and methodological terms, there are also tensions in emancipatory aspirations that propose people with learning difficulties should 'set the research agenda, collaborate on the design and development of strategies, collect some of the data, contribute to its analysis and share in the dissemination process', and in recognising that, for some, the 'cognitive and linguistic demands of such activity prevent the full involvement of all people with learning difficult but that it is important that they contribute their views' (Lewis and Porter, 2004, p 3).

While it has been recognised that new or more flexible methods need to be used among these participants in order for them to express their views in different ways, they will also sometimes require substantial support from researchers and advocates, for example, in order to participate effectively and in ways that they might want. Self-advocacy movements/organisations have been critical here in facilitating the engagement of people with learning difficulties in research, but it is also recognised that greater 'cross-fertilisation' (Kiernan, 1999, p 47) between traditional and participatory models of research are also needed. In short, including people with learning difficulties in research puts the spotlight on research methods and research praxis in ways that demand expertise, understanding and mutuality in research management and in researcher–participant relationships.

Emerging participatory methods in learning difficulty research

Even though it is recognised that advances have been made in disability and learning difficulty research using participatory and/or emancipatory approaches and methods, and even though research has been conducted by people with learning difficulties themselves, both from within and outside the academy and as part of the self-advocacy movement (see, for example, Aspis, 2000; Townson et al, 2004), it is also clear that research with and by people with profound learning difficulties is relatively sparse. The reasons for this may seem obvious given what has been discussed so far with respect to the challenges involved more broadly of including excluded or multiply 'vulnerable' people in research, and it is these challenges that may, to some extent, serve to deter researchers (and particularly non-disabled researchers within the academy, for example) from engaging with such participants in more inclusive ways. Thus, the often more complex ethical considerations involved, issues relating to access and perceived difficulties of managing and negotiating researcher–participant relationships (especially in research that involves non-disabled and/or non-specialist researchers) are all pertinent issues in learning difficulty research. In addition, without a doubt, research with people with learning difficulties – and particularly those with severe or profound difficulties or impairments – requires particular skills, expertise and insight on the part of researchers themselves, and particularly when undertaking PR or aspirant 'emancipatory' projects that have social change objectives.

It is also important to acknowledge that, because of the diversity across learning difficulty populations (see Stalker, 1998), people with profound problems, challenges or impairments may not be able to undertake research themselves, or they may even be left out of studies that attempt to promote emancipation and autonomy. As has been suggested, this can be explained to some extent through the use of inappropriate methods or failings on the part of researchers to use methods that are tailored to individual needs (that therefore recognise the diversity among individuals). Indeed, this is evident even in qualitative studies that claim to be participatory or emancipatory, but which still rely heavily on methods that demand either verbal contributions from participants or rely on third party interpretations – of, for example, the behaviours or gestures of people with learning difficulties (Nind refers to these as 'augmentative and alternative communication' [2008, p 10]). Thus, evidence of participatory approaches that are flexible and adaptive and that promote 'voice' in whatever context (visual, artistic, creative, and so on) still tends very much to be the exception. In Nind's (2008) review of PR on children and adults with learning difficulties, for example, the majority of methods described relied on verbal or written contributions from participants, including interviews, focus groups, questionnaires/surveys, and life story/narrative research. Other methods also relied on third party or proxy interventions to assess participants' attitudes, behaviours, and so on (for example, ethnographic and participant observation studies). Methods that did not rely on participants' verbal or written input were less common, although two approaches were highlighted specifically that relied on other sensory methods such as visual research and the use of cue cards as prompts in research 'conversations' or during different data collection phases of studies.

Visual methods in learning difficult research

In Ollerton and Horsfall's (2013) PhotoVoice study on the rights of people with learning difficulties, the authors purposively combined inclusive research (see Walmsley and Johnson, 2003) with PAR, describing their approach as 'inclusive participatory action research' (IPAR) (Ollerton and Horsfall, 2013, p 620), in which people with learning difficulties were given disposable cameras to capture and identify barriers to self-determination. The method was chosen because 'it does not presume the ability to read or write', and because it gave participants 'the right to name the world as they saw it' (pp 620-1), using 'accessible' and 'rigorous' methods. While participatory PhotoVoice methods are not commonly used in learning difficulty research (or perhaps not as commonly used as they should be), among the first proponents of the method were Booth and Booth who used the PhotoVoice method with people with learning difficulties because,

> It puts people in charge of how they represent themselves and how they depict their situation. The process challenges the politics of representation by shifting control over the means for documenting lives from the powerful to the powerless, the expert to the lay-person, the professional to the client, the bureaucrat to the citizen, the observer to the observed. (2003, p 432)

There are therefore a number of important reasons why alternative, visual PR methods such as these are more appropriate when working with people with learning difficulties – they prioritise the needs of individuals; they facilitate and promote different versions of (visual) 'voice'; and they offer accessible ways of including people who might otherwise be left out of research studies because they are deemed too 'difficult' or challenging to include. Furthermore, when used as part of a multi-method approach, these kinds of techniques can also mean that the views and perspectives of people with learning difficulties, even those who experience profound or severe cognitive and communicative problems, may be included in general population studies where methods are designed and used that are flexible and that can accommodate the needs of different participant groups. In this way, learning difficulty research can also be located in 'mainstream' studies that use both conventional and 'alternative' methods of data collection. The only prerequisite in these kinds of approaches is that researchers need to be aware of them in the first instance – of what is possible in methods terms – and also need to think carefully about their relevance and value when planning participatory projects with people who don't want, or who are unable, to participate in studies that use more conventional methods.

The main advantage, then, of using participatory photographic methods such as PhotoVoice with people with learning difficulties is that it removes the need to rely on participants' verbal contributions and promotes the use of other, more accessible, sensorial methods; thus, it does not make presumptions or assumptions about participants' willingness or capacities to read or write. A further benefit to using visual methods in these contexts is that they promote identity (through experience and 'voice'), and both the rights and competency of participants. Chappell and colleagues (2001, p 48) argue, for example, that there is a pressing need to use methods that 'reject a deficit approach to learning difficulties' and that place a 'clear emphasis on experiential issues' (p 47) and thus emphasise both rights and competency. Ollerton and Horsfall's (2013) participatory study of people with learning difficulties embraced both these aspects through the use of the *Convention on the Rights of Persons with Disabilities* (CRPWD, 2008) specifically as in inclusive PAR tool (or IPAR, as discussed earlier). Through the technique of 'PhotoVoice', the authors challenged the barriers people with learning difficulties faced with respect to their rights as citizens (on public transport, in 'group homes', and so on) by presenting photographic images of these in situ, so to speak, to policy makers and practitioners. The photograph of the iron bar door preventing access to the kitchen in the group home is a particularly telling example here (Ollerton and Horsfall, 2013, p 622), and shows how participants were forbidden access to everyday activities (in this case, cooking) that non-disabled people, for example, would not have to face.

Including and working with people with learning difficulties in photographic research, and especially in studies where participants are also responsible for data collection, as co-researchers, also serves to emphasise the competencies of participants – as both researchers and as photographers. This was one of the main aims of the Social and Therapeutic Horticulture (STH) study with people with learning difficulties that used photographic participation methods as part of a broader, multi-method project (Sempik et al, 2005),[3] and was also Booth and Booth's (2003) objective in their pioneering study of mothers with learning difficulties. The authors noted the contributions visual methods such as PhotoVoice could make to the emancipatory ideals of the social model, and specifically, the way in which PhotoVoice as a participatory technique helped to crystallise issues in ways that are less abstract and more appropriate to the styles of thinking of people with learning difficulties. Furthermore, giving participants cameras was seen as an important action ('we "take" photos after all'; Booth and Booth, 2013, p 3), in terms of prioritising empowerment over questions about acquiescence that are often raised in other kinds of methods with these groups. The authors also argued that 'it allows people the opportunity to exercise choice as competent participants in the research process' (Booth and Booth, 2003, p 3).

Similarly, one of the key outcomes of the participatory phase of the STH study with people with learning difficulties (Sempik et al, 2005; see also Aldridge, 2007) was that the photographic method itself presented participants – as co-researchers, as photographers – in ways that challenged conventional or stereotypical perceptions of learning difficulty:

> The use of photography in this case emphasised the capacity of vulnerable respondents rather than their incapacity and allowed us to move away from a pathological perspective that tends to focus on the deficits of people with learning disabilities. The emphasis on pathology here is widely recognised. Lakin (1997), for example, has argued that, "it has been assumed that 'cognitive impairments' – which diagnosticians determine based on performance in vocabulary, memory, mathematics and abstract reasoning – are total impairments, pervasively diminishing everything those so 'afflicted' can do (p 4).'" (Aldridge, 2007, p 12)

So it can be seen that in constructing these visual narratives of identity and experience, and collectivising these data in studies that use these kinds of methods as they grow in number and value, different perspectives on the lives and contributions of people with learning difficulties can be developed. In this way, while individual participatory projects may be limited in terms of realising their emancipatory and social change objectives in the short term, transformations as a result of these studies may occur over time and in more fundamental ways.

Furthermore, as interest in, and use of, participatory visual methods such as PhotoVoice also develops, so does recognition of their importance and reliability as research methodologies in and of themselves, as well as their relevance and applicability among diverse participant groups (including excluded, marginalised or multiply vulnerable populations), particularly at the point, as Booth and Booth (2003, p 432) state, 'in people's lives where biography and society intersect'. Indeed, based on their own experience of using PhotoVoice with mothers with learning difficulties, the authors propose three main goals (and advantages) of the PhotoVoice method: it facilitates and encourages participant reflection on, and exploration of, personal experience and identity; it promotes 'personal strength and common cause with like others' through group discussions about the photographs that have been produced; and it presents these experiences and identities in visual form in order to educate and inform others such as policy makers and practitioners.

However, a number of challenges and dilemmas present themselves when using less conventional, participatory visual methods such as these, and particularly among participants who experience severe or profound learning difficulties. It is important that these challenges are addressed, as well as the limitations of PR with respect to learning difficulty research, and these matters are particularly important when considering the challenges involved in using less conventional visual methods among participant groups that are generally also more likely to be excluded from research participation.

Challenges and considerations in participatory research with people with learning difficulties

Some of the fundamental questions that need to be addressed when considering these challenges are how far participatory methods (including participatory visual methods) can achieve genuinely emancipatory objectives when working with people with *profound* learning difficulties (or looked at another way, is genuine emancipation a realistic goal in this context?). What are the interpretive, representational and analytical dilemmas involved in PR with people with profound learning difficulties? Are there specific ethical considerations and requirements when using PR in these contexts, and particularly when using participatory visual methods? As has been discussed, the key principles and objectives in PR are reciprocity and mutuality in researcher–participant relationships, and in 'emancipatory' research (at the 'top end' of the Participatory Model – see Chapter Six, Figure 6.1) the inclusion of participants at all stages of the research process lead to social change outcomes.

However, to some extent, these principles and aims are inevitably compromised in research that includes people with profound learning difficulties, especially when participants experience cognitive, communicative or multiple impairments, and it is important not to deny the impact of these in research processes and outcomes and for participants themselves. As Richardson argues, 'it would be folly for research to disregard the limitations arriving from [impairments]' (2000, p 1391). In considering the use of visual techniques, and photographic participation and PhotoVoice methods specifically, with people with profound learning difficulties as alternative ways of facilitating and eliciting (visual) 'voice', two observations are notable here. First, while PhotoVoice relies on participants taking charge and ownership of data and data collection phases in research as photographers (which is both significant and of value in participatory terms), it also relies on discussions or 'conversations' between participants (and between participants and researchers) based on the data produced, either individually or in groups (see, for example, Booth and Booth, 2003).

This aspect of the method inevitably calls into question the principle and intention of using the visual as an alternative to verbal contribution.[4] Second, so often methodological discussions in studies that use photo participation or PhotoVoice techniques either do not indicate the extent or severity of the learning difficulty experienced by participants involved, or they mainly include people with 'mild to moderate' learning difficulties – in Jurowski and Paul-Ward's (2007) study of the disparities in health promotion for people with learning difficulties, and Ollerton and Horsfall's (2013) study of the barriers people with learning difficulties face in terms of their human rights, both included participants with 'mild to moderate' learning difficulties. In Booth and Booth's (2003) PhotoVoice study of mothers with learning difficulties, it is not made clear the extent or severity of the learning difficulties experienced by participants, although it is noted that they were able to engage in group conversations using the photographic data as a starting point for these.

While these studies emphasise emancipatory and social change objectives and outcomes, they do not offer any concrete solutions to using these or other kinds of participatory methods with people who have profound or multiple learning difficulties, in which case it is necessary to acknowledge and accept that in some cases or specific instances, PR with people with profound learning difficulties will inevitably have to rely on close alliances between participants and non-disabled researchers. Some argue, however, that this is both important and in some cases necessary, as long as researchers have the appropriate skills and knowledge to work within PR frameworks and understand the needs of excluded or multiply vulnerable people (and specifically in photographic research that 'exposes' human subjects to visual scrutiny or focus). Chappell and colleagues (2001, p 42) recognise, for example, that, 'people with learning difficulties need sympathetic non-disabled researchers who can use their position to articulate the experience of people with learning difficulties to the outside world' (at the same time, it needs to be acknowledged that this would inevitably compromise some of the key principles of a genuinely 'emancipatory' approach, as outlined and proposed in the social model of disability).

The importance and value of research relationships

It is commonly accepted that establishing good and effective researcher–participant relationships is an essential 'first step towards eliciting the views of people with learning difficulties' (Lewis and Porter, 2004, p 195). Such relationships are even more vital to the success of PR when working with people with profound learning difficulties, and especially in their relationships with non-disabled researchers. In such instances, I would argue that these kinds of relationships are not just a first step in research processes, but are fundamental to the entire research endeavour, and to successful (even transformative) outcomes for participants. Thus, an essential factor or consideration in successfully and effectively planning, designing and implementing research with people with profound learning difficulties is the relationships researchers build with participants and with others who work with them and support them as and when necessary. These relationships are also key in ensuring participants are engaged in research in ways that are appropriate and that facilitate collaboration and mutuality as far as possible. However, ensuring and achieving these outcomes will depend on a number of critical factors – for example, on researchers' assessments of participants' willingness and ability to participate on their own terms, and in accordance with relevant ethical procedures, and on how successfully researchers manage and negotiate their own roles as enablers or facilitators and as professionals in their own right who have particular and necessary skills, knowledge and roles to play.

Rather than itemise or address these issues in turn as individual topics for discussion or consideration, as is common practice in discussions or reviews of research methods, it is perhaps preferable, and more illuminating, to illustrate these matters through direct example, that is, from research studies that have successfully addressed all of these issues in the field, so to speak, using PR methods and techniques. While a number of research studies with people with learning difficulties have been discussed so far in this chapter, it is useful at this point to draw further on these as well as on the specific example of the STH study to illustrate the ways in which researcher–participant relationships can be managed successfully in PR with people with *profound* learning difficulties, and the process by which research ethics intersect and are managed using PR methods. Drawing on specific examples in this way also serves to address a recognised gap in the field of learning difficulty research and in disability studies more generally, as well as recognising that 'while there is a growing literature about the values and principles underlying work in this field, particularly in relation to PR, it seems that less has been written examining the specific issues encountered in empirical studies' (Stalker, 1998, p 17).

Participatory photographic research: the Social and Therapeutic Horticulture study

The broader objectives of the STH study were to explore the experiences and needs of a range of excluded or vulnerable groups, including people with mental and physical health problems, those who had been the victims of abuse and torture, and people with learning difficulties. While structured and semi-structured interviews were used with the majority of the participants in the study, different methods were required when working with the clients of the STH gardening projects who had profound learning difficulties (Thrive and STH staff referred to those who attended the STH projects as 'clients'). Photographic participation techniques were chosen because evidence of their successful use among these populations had been noted elsewhere, and also because it was recognised that methods were needed among specific learning disabled groups that did not rely on their verbal contributions. The participatory approach was also developed as a result of visits to STH projects and discussions with staff about the needs of particular clients, and thus the need for alternative, more flexible participatory methods were identified at this initial stage. The underpinning participatory philosophy was based on what Chappell et al (2001, p 41) describe as 'the notion of the sympathetic and committed researcher striving to improve the lives of people with learning difficulties'; the intention was therefore that the research would facilitate more equitable research relationships, would recognise the rights of people with learning difficulties to be consulted about participation, and that the 'quality and relevance' of the research would be improved by their direct involvement in the process (Stalker, 1998, p 6).

Furthermore, in initial meetings with project staff and clients and through observations and researcher assessments it was clear that the client group included individual participants with such profound communicative difficulties that identifying and developing methods that did not rely on verbal contributions would be essential (see Aldridge, 2007). Thus, methods were adapted according to the specific needs of this participant group – using different sensory-based methods that were easier for them to use and that did not rely on verbal input or memory performance (see Aldridge and Dearden, 2013). Aspects of the photographic participation method also mirrored Goodley's (1996) 'life plan' approach, to some extent, where visual representations were used to construct narratives of people with learning difficulties.

Establishing and developing research relationships

Nind (2008, p 6) argues that, 'A primary feature of ethics protocols in qualitative research is the quality of the relationship between researcher and participants.' In one sense, this was the starting point from which ethical protocols were developed and established in the STH study, but these also influenced, and at the same time were determined by, the nature and importance of *ongoing* relationships and, in the broader context of the study, with the ethics of participation and representation. In establishing and maintaining relationships with participants (and with project staff)[5] at the STH gardening projects, the process not only involved initial meetings with them through a series of project visits, but also taking part in project activities and working *alongside* participants. This involved the research team participating in gardening and social activities, meal times and travelling with participants (to other garden sites as part of contract work) as part of the process of *sharing* and *getting to know one another*. During this important initial phase of the research, it was also possible to assess and establish participants' willingness and ability to take part in the study – and therefore their willingness and capacity to give consent – as an essential first step in the participatory process.

In conventional qualitative studies it is necessary to pay close attention to ethical issues and requirements when working with excluded or marginalised groups, but it is especially important when working with people with profound learning difficulties or multiple impairments. When using visual methods in such contexts, these matters are equally critical but often made more complicated by the nature of the method itself. In the main this is because using PR methods to address and overcome barriers to participation – through the shift from methods that rely on verbal contributions to those that rely on visual input from participants, for example – presents further ethical challenges with respect to negotiating and managing issues such as confidentiality and consent procedures (as Donaldson argues, 'designing confidentiality and informed consent procedures that take into account photography's loss of privacy will be especially troublesome' [2001, p 4]). These issues will be even more pertinent when working with participants whose cognitive impairments may mean they do not fully understand these concepts.

While obtaining informed consent in research is both a moral and legal obligation and is particularly important in learning difficulty research, it is possible that PR methods themselves can help in managing and meeting ethical requirements more broadly, in establishing ethical protocols and in ensuring that the research is in the 'best interests' of participants themselves. In the STH study, access to participants and agreement that the research was in their best interests had already been discussed and agreed prior to the fieldwork phase. Both the research study partner and staff at individual STH projects across the UK had extensive experience of working with diverse groups of vulnerable and multiply vulnerable clients and were best placed to decide the types of research that would serve these clients' best interests. Furthermore, in many cases, projects were supported by advisory or steering groups, which included client representatives who had a say in project planning and priorities (including research priorities). Furthermore, following discussions with staff from the partner organisation and individual projects, it was clear that the participatory photographic method was seen as a positive strategy in extending the opportunities and capacities for people with profound learning difficulties to be involved. Without these methods such opportunities would be limited or denied, and thus the views or perspectives of these clients about their experiences of STH interventions would not be represented at all.

Ethical issues: consent

Assessing participants' abilities to understand ethical concepts and to give informed consent is a more complex process when participants have profound learning difficulties, but is also an essential element of the relationship-building process. In the STH study a more holistic approach was adopted to research ethics and to consent procedures specifically. This process involved working closely with participants in communicating information about the project itself and about their participation. It was also necessary to discuss and obtain consent and assent from participants and/or those who had legal responsibility or guardianship for them, where appropriate, and to take into account the views and perspectives of project staff who worked closely with participants on a regular basis about ethical and consent issues. As part of this holistic process, social and environmental factors were also important considerations in terms of recognising the safety and familiarity of the project environment for participants (the fact that for many, the gardening projects were one of the few spaces in their lives where they could participate in social and/or physical activities on their own terms), and that it was important for meetings and discussions about the research, and ethical procedures, to take place in this environment. Specific strategies for obtaining as well as monitoring consent and assent included repeated explanations about the research and the photographic method in one-to-one encounters with participants and in the presence of project workers or someone they knew well and trusted; observing responses such as positive indicators of consent/assent, levels of non-verbal and verbal responses, gestures, body language and so on – these responses were also checked with project staff and or significant others in their lives. As Nind (2008, p 8) observes, 'it is often family members and advocates who can best advise on these issues.'

It is important that ethical issues relating to confidentiality, consent and participation more broadly (including the right to refuse consent or withdraw from participation) are also considered as part of an *ongoing process* throughout the duration of research projects. In the STH study, the photographic method itself was used as an adaptive and dedicated PR technique and, to some extent, as a measure or indicator of ethical and participatory procedures. These aspects of the STH study, as well as the further ways in which participants were involved in more collaborative ways, are described below.

Confidentiality/anonymity

It was agreed from the outset that none of the photographs taken by participants with learning difficulties would be used that included images of other participants. Photographs of other people would only be used where consent had been obtained. In this way, the anonymity of participants was preserved.[6] While privacy and anonymity issues are critical in terms of ensuring ethical considerations and requirements are met in research processes (and these are even more important when dealing with the potential loss of privacy photographic methods present), the use of the photographic participation method in the STH study was intended as an aid to participation more than as a method of eliciting data that might be sensitive or difficult to manage ethically. Participants were only asked to take photographs on site at STH gardening projects of aspects that were important to them (see also Booth and Booth, 2003). In this way, the method was a way of demonstrating unique insight into their lives, and as 'a culturally fashioned extension of the senses ... so that it provides a potential to question, arouse curiosity, tell in different voices, or see through different eyes from beyond' (Radley and Taylor, 2003, p 79).

'Ownership' of data

Participants 'owned' their own photographic data in that their first names were attributed to these images in any outputs from the study and in the gallery of images presented on the research project website as well as on gardening project websites (with participants' consent/ permission); all participants were also given printed copies of their photographs to keep. Importantly, this process also helped promote participants' competencies as researchers and as photographers, and was a fundamental aim of, and outcome from, the study. Booth and Booth's study of mothers with learning difficulties (2003, p 440) generated similar outputs and findings in that the photographic albums that were produced offered 'insight into the lives of individual mothers with learning difficulties at the same time as they illuminate the collective experiences of these mothers as a group.'

Selecting images: 'telling' the visual story

The printed copies of participants' photographs were used in further visits and meetings with them that included reviewing the photographs and observing responses. In this way, the photographs themselves served as useful cues or prompts in these review sessions. In some cases participants who were able wanted to describe or respond verbally to selected images (and where possible these were used as captions to the photographs). As Gilbert argues, people with learning difficulties may not use the language of data analysis, but they are often still able to 'highlight elements that they [find] interesting' (2004, p 303). During this phase, once again, responses to the data were observed and checked (including with project staff who knew participants well); where participants were excited or seemed happy with the photographs (also observed through gestures, body language, and so on) this was then seen as assent to continue with the fieldwork at this stage. In this way participants had some power of redress – images would not be used where participants responded negatively during the checking process. Content and thematic analyses were conducted on the final selection of photographic data so that the findings could contribute to the broader objectives of the study.

Representation

While the STH study did not, and to some degree simply could not, aspire to a fully 'emancipatory' objective in that participants with profound learning difficulties were not included at all stages of the research process, one of the fundamental aims of the project was to ensure that their views or perspectives were represented and included within the broader aims of the study. Thus, the aim was to present participants' photographs in the form of photographic galleries or albums online, as they were (attributed by name but without any interpretive or explanatory caption written by third parties; see also the discussion in Chapter Two), as well as include them in these ways as part of more conventional outputs from the study, for example, in the end of project report, in academic and professional journal articles, conference papers and so on, in which the photographic data were contextualised. The photographs have also been used in more creative ways as photographs with artistic merit in their own right (on the covers of books, on the walls of offices in horticultural organisations, universities and so on). Using the photographs in these ways, in ensuring that the images themselves were always attributed (and thus 'owned' by the participant-photographers) ensured that it was clear whose (visual) 'voice' or narrative was being presented (see Booth, 1996). Emphasising attribution and ownership of the photographic data thus not only conferred competency on participants, and emphasised their roles as active participant-photographers, but more broadly (from a health and social care perspective, for example), it helped challenge the *recipient of care* perspective where 'service users only have freedom to act within that dependency frame and not therefore upon it' (Richardson, 2000, p 1,391).

Feedback and actions

Lewis and Porter (2004, p 193) propose that 'a fundamental concern that underpins PR is to ensure reciprocity in the activity'. One of the important ways in which such reciprocity can be extended in PR methods is by ensuring participants have access to and benefit from the findings of research. When working with people with profound learning difficulties, feedback will need to be presented in ways they can understand and appreciate. In the STH study findings from the research were presented in an easy language format summary, using pictorial images, as well as the photographic images taken by the participants themselves. The photographic data were also used to illustrate and highlight specific issues relating to findings and messages from the broader objectives of the STH study (in conferences, discussions with stakeholders and so on). Similarly, in Ollerton and Horsfall's (2013) rights-based study involving people with learning difficulties, participants used photographic data themselves as evidence of the barriers to their rights in letters and other communication with key stakeholders, policy makers and so on. In some cases, researchers helped in the preparation of these letters and in further communications with stakeholders. These actions support the principles and objectives of an emancipatory approach that involves participants at all stages of the research process. However, in many instances, involving people with *profound* learning difficulties (that include severe cognitive and communicative impairments, for example) in these ways is not always possible.

While these kinds of emancipatory objectives may thus be just out of reach when considering participants' full involvement in research, even in those studies that facilitate engagement and inclusion in more flexible and appropriate ways, the same arguments may also be levied when research includes close and sometimes necessary alliances between participants with learning difficulties and non-disabled researchers. Although in some cases boundaries may be crossed with respect to researchers' roles as investigators and as activists, some have argued that researchers cannot be sufficiently 'objective' to engage in genuine activism (see Chappell et al, 2001). Others who subscribe more rigidly to the social model argue that the only genuinely emancipatory research project is one in which participants take full control, and thus the role of the researcher (as investigator, activist or aspirant activist) is negated. Of course, it is often the case that these essentially intellectual arguments and discourses themselves often take place within the academy, and are led by people who are not learning disabled themselves, and so these types of arguments become somewhat moot without input on these matters from people for whom the outcomes of these debates have most consequence – people with learning difficulties themselves.

Some concluding observations

When reviewing the range and diversity of research that has been conducted with vulnerable individuals, groups and communities (and particularly when assessing these in terms of their location within participatory frameworks or models), the distinction between different approaches in PR become more clear. However, in disability research and in research on people with learning difficulties, these distinctions have, to some extent, become more divergent as a consequence of the drive towards 'emancipatory' research in disability studies. To some extent, this has led to the absence or belatedness of learning difficulty research and perspectives within social model theory, research and practice. However, as has been shown, a number of important advances have been made in the field of learning difficulty research itself and in new government initiatives, policies and laws, as well as within the field of disability rights, activism and self-advocacy.

As is often the case, however, what is proposed in theory and in practice is often distinct from the reality – or the 'multiple constructions of reality' (Chevalier and Buckles, 2013, p 38) – of people's lives. In many respects, this conflict or tension is mirrored in different, and often conflicting, perspectives on and methods of working with people with learning difficulties. This is not just because epistemological debates, for example, will always or inevitably conflict or divert at particular points, or over certain issues, but also because in many respects people with profound learning difficulties or multiple problems/impairments present equally diverse challenges, as well as opportunities for working with them in ways that promote their best interests.

In terms of theoretical and epistemological debates, these can be summarised in the dilemmas of identity and dualism and what these mean for people with learning difficulties themselves. Such is the diversity, or lack of homogeneity, among people with learning difficulties that there will inevitably be conflict between if and how they relate to a disability identity, for example, and whether such an identity takes full and necessary account of their independence, impairment or self-advocacy. These issues will also be pertinent when contemplating or planning research with people with learning difficulties and the best and most appropriate ways of working with them, as well as the type of research they conduct themselves.

For researchers contemplating empirical investigations with these groups, participatory approaches should be considered from the outset, and the most appropriate methods within PR that suit the specific needs of participants with learning difficulties. In some cases, more conventional qualitative PR methods will be sufficient. In other cases where participants have profound learning difficulties or multiple impairments, methods that do not rely on verbal competency, but that emphasise and promote genuine participation in other ways, will be required. While these issues need to be addressed prior to the commencement of research investigations, and particularly in planning and making decisions about methodological choices, many of these considerations can only be properly addressed through consultation with participants themselves and through the relationships that develop between them and researchers as studies progress.

Visual methods represent an obvious choice when working with people with profound learning difficulties because they help address and overcome issues of verbal competency, the need for abstract reasoning or recall and problematic questions about acquiescence and compliance among these groups (see Booth and Booth, 2003). They can also serve to emphasise and promote competency, control and ownership in and of research processes and thus help to counteract deficiency stereotypes so often associated with people with profound learning and communicative difficulties.

We can therefore see how consideration of the role and value of participatory methods in research can both address practical decisions about 'how best to' achieve participatory objectives, as well as contribute different perspectives on epistemological and ideological debates. The processes involved in working within a PR framework provide opportunities to reflect on and identify the ways in which participatory principles and objectives are made manifest – that is, how these translate into research practice – and thus how they can also help reconcile or bridge the divide between different theoretical perspectives or epistemologies. For example, there may be some tension, and indeed, distinction, between participatory and 'emancipatory' research methods from a social model perspective and from perspectives and theories in other disciplines and fields. However, when considering in detail the research processes involved when working inclusively with people with learning difficulties, for example, we can see how participatory methods themselves can help to interpose between or even reconcile these distinctions.

As has been shown, using visual methods such as PhotoVoice or photographic participation techniques can have important and necessary transformative outcomes for participants even if they aren't involved at every stage of the research process. Such transformations may not, or indeed, should not, be limited to social change outcomes in the form of policy shifts or adaptations or changes in law (although, of course, these are also important outcomes), nor do they, or should they, only occur in the short term as a result of evidence from specific research studies. In many respects, such transformations can be, and often are, more nuanced and less immediate than this. The full implications of some of the studies described and discussed in this chapter, for example, may not yet be known. Ollerton and Horsfall's (2013) study identified the human rights barriers experienced by people with learning difficulties in 'group homes', on public transport and so on. While some actions were identified and changes occurred on the conclusion of the study, the full impact or consequences of this research for people with learning difficulties themselves may not yet be felt or fully realised. With respect to the STH research, the participatory visual phase of the multi-method STH study did not include specific end of project actions for participants with learning difficulties, but as part of the broader study, the messages for health and social care were clear and have subsequently resulted in new plans for using STH for patients with mental health problems and learning difficulties in the NHS (see Sustain, 2013).

These kinds of transformations can thus occur as a result of collective datasets that tell the same or similar stories, and can thus provide more 'convincing' or 'credible' evidence in policy and practice terms, for example. While the number of studies that use less conventional participatory methods with people with learning difficulties are somewhat sparse, considered in the context of research with other excluded, marginalised or vulnerable groups, as well as in the context of health or disability studies more broadly, then their messages perhaps become more convincing at a collective level; and it is also here where less conventional participatory methods gain prominence.

Furthermore, there are advantages to be gained in ensuring participatory methods are also included in large-scale, multi-method research studies that include marginalised or vulnerable participants or, put another way, that research methods can be sufficiently flexible and accommodating to address the needs of these participants in broader, 'mainstream' studies. Additionally, research studies, and methods themselves, should be able to accommodate and include marginalised or vulnerable groups when they occur in randomly selected samples. In fact, it could be argued that to some extent the test or measure of the impact of new epistemologies, movements and understanding about social exclusion and the needs of vulnerable groups (including people with learning difficulties) is that these groups occur, and can be accommodated in general population studies, and not be distinct or separate from them.

A further reason why it is important for marginalised or vulnerable people to be included in more conventional, 'mainstream' studies that adopt multi- or mixed-method approaches is because such people cannot always 'speak for' or represent themselves, nor are they necessarily able, or given opportunities to conduct research themselves. Sometimes alliances are needed with researchers who may have broader objectives outside the confines, say, of learning difficulty or disability research. The benefits for these groups of being involved in studies that have different and more catholic aims and intentions are that they may be able to more readily accommodate a diversity of needs using methods that are flexible and adaptive. When considering the advantages of participatory visual methods among people with learning difficulties in the STH study, the intention was not to discuss or replicate the findings from this research in their entirety (these are recorded and discussed in detail elsewhere; see Sempik et al, 2005); rather, the aim was to demonstrate the efficacy of working inclusively with people with profound learning difficulties as part of a multi-method investigation. The contribution of the participants themselves was manifold, not least in the ways they were able to provide rich, extensive and illuminating visual data that continue to be relevant and of value today. Thus, the emphasis in the study was on individual experiential perspectives *as well as* the broader aspects of social inclusion, underpinned by a firm commitment to being accountable to participants with learning difficulties in the research as part of much larger, multi-method endeavour (see Chappell et al, 2001).

It is argued that it is imperative that we continue to look for innovative or more creative methods when working with marginalised or excluded groups such as those that have been described and discussed in this chapter. Although much has been learned about the needs of people with learning difficulties in participatory or inclusive research, it is equally important, therefore, that we continue to develop different, creative methods and relationships in research in order to expand our horizons of what is possible.

FOUR

Participatory research with victims of abuse and trauma: women victims-survivors of domestic violence

Introduction

With respect to this expansive vision of what is achievable in PR with vulnerable or marginalised groups, and especially those who may be defined as multiply vulnerable, this chapter focuses on participatory approaches with victims of abuse and trauma with a particular focus on women victims-survivors of domestic violence. This chapter also considers some of the important reasons why participants such as these require research methods that emphasise personal autonomy and agency, drawing in particular on narrative methods and intensive participatory narrative techniques. Using the example of an ongoing participatory narrative writing project with unsupported women victims-survivors of domestic violence,[1] the chapter shows what is achievable in PR methods terms among participant groups who are largely isolated or hidden.

Narrative research is relevant to the focus of the discussion in this chapter (and, indeed, to the book as a whole; see the Introduction and Chapter One), and to participatory methods and approaches, not simply because of its long history in the social sciences, but because of its emphasis on individual, 'insider' perspectives (see Gilbert, 2004, p 301). As Gilbert states,

> Booth and Booth (1996) emphasised the difference between interview research and narrative research, with the former providing material for the researcher's narrative. In contrast, narrative research enables individuals to tell their stories. (2004, p 301)

The participatory elements of the narrative research discussed in this chapter with respect to the participatory narrative research (PNR) study with unsupported women victims-survivors[2] of domestic violence are important and necessary additions to the narrative approach. This is because they help to reinforce the idea – illustrated through the PNR study and the specific narrative example included in the second half of this chapter – that it is not just the telling of the story or narrative that is important, but also the degree of ownership and control among participants themselves over the narrative method and its construction, and the way in which this is presented (as opposed to re-presented) through authorial 'voice'.

Victims of violence, abuse and trauma

In the late 1980s, Gondolf (1988) identified a range of psychological consequences of domestic violence for women, such as, for example, low self-esteem, depression, self-blame, lack of autonomy and fear of separation from their abusers, as critical factors that underscore their vulnerability. However, he also argued that these outcomes should be considered as part of the adjustment process in initiating help-seeking activity among women. Nevertheless, such adverse or harmful reactions to abuse and violence can also be considered as understandable responses to traumatic shock, that is, to extreme or prolonged stress and/or trauma, in the same way victims of other forms of trauma are affected – the impacts of violent assault, child abuse, conflict and war, for example (see Herman, 1992; see also Hughes and Jones, 2000).

In clinical and diagnostic terms, definitions of trauma focus on human responses to physical injury or threat of such. For example, the American Psychiatric Association (APA) defines traumatic stress as, 'when a person experienced, witnessed, or was confronted with an event or events that involved actual or threatened death or serious injury or a threat to the physical integrity of self or others' (APA, 2001, p 467). In therapeutic terms, victims of trauma include those who have experienced natural disaster, combat, kidnapping or criminal victimisation, violence and abuse. Describing their work with child and adult victims of abuse, Pritchard and Sainsbury (2004, p 11) also refer to a range of traumatic experiences among their clients as a result of physical or sexual abuse, neglect and fear, 'but all arising from the degrading and dehumanising behaviour of other people, and all leading to an erosion of self-esteem and confidence' (and which the authors address specifically through the use of creative writing practices as a way of helping participants 'regain control over their feelings and, thus, their lives'; Pritchard and Sainsbury, 2004, p 11; see also the discussion later in Chapter Five).

It is often helpful, then, to consider the impacts of domestic violence on women in the same way as victims of other kinds of trauma experience harrowing episodes or events, and thus also to understand and conceptualise the nature of their 'vulnerability' in these terms. Evidence shows, for example, that women who experience domestic violence from an early age and when the violence is severe and enduring are more likely to experience symptoms of post-traumatic stress disorder (PTSD). As Hughes and Jones (2000, p 4) note:

> Posttraumatic Stress Disorder (PTSD) has been diagnosed most commonly in rape, child sexual abuse, and war victims. More recently, studies have found battered women meet the criteria for PTSD. The severity of the violence, the duration of exposure, early-age onset, and the victim's cognitive assessment of the violence (perceived degree of threat, predictability, and controllability) exacerbate the symptoms.

However, while such a perspective is important, it must also be remembered that considering and treating domestic violence and its impact on women using only a strict psychiatric or medical model may not necessarily be appropriate. Some have argued, for example, that in doing so there is a danger of pathologising women, making domestic violence simply a mental health problem – and thus, a personal or unique vulnerability – and as a consequence, potentially further victimising women (see Romito, 2008). It is therefore also appropriate to understand women's domestic violence victimisation as a consequence of the dehumanising behaviour of others – when such behaviour is abusive in nature and traumatic in its consequences – as well as a form of structural oppression. This helps us understand and contextualise the reasons for women's vulnerability or marginalisation in these contexts in extrinsic or systemic terms, rather than occurring solely as a result of an innate or unique psychological condition (see Larkin, 2009).

In this broader context, both epistemologically and in terms of health and social care discourses and practices, as well as in international research evidence and legislation, women's experiences of, and responses to, domestic violence are described and addressed in macro global discourses on violence against women more generally, and include, for example, women as victims (and survivors) of rape and sexual assault, 'honour' killing, female genital mutilation (FGM), child abuse and sex trafficking (see Hoff, 2001; Romito, 2008). As Ellsberg and Heise (2005, p 11) state, all of these kinds of violence against women are now 'recognized as a legitimate human rights issue and as a significant threat to women's health and well-being.'

Prevalence and impact of domestic violence on women

Global, population-based surveys reveal the prevalence of domestic violence worldwide. A World Bank study in 1993 showed that violence against women caused more death and disability across the globe (among women aged 15-44) than war, cancer, malaria and traffic accidents combined. More recently, the World Health Organization *Multi-country study on women's health and violence against women* (WHO, 2005) showed that '15-71% of women experience physical and/or sexual violence by an intimate partner at some point in their lives.' In the UK alone, research in the last two decades has found that one incidence of domestic violence is reported to the police every minute, and domestic violence accounts for one quarter of all recorded violent crime (Dodd et al, 2004).

While the latest national statistics from the UK on domestic violence appear to suggest a reduction in the number of domestic violence incidents experienced by women between 1993 and 2010, consideration of both the methods of data collection and the ways in which these data are interpreted suggest that the opposite may, in fact, be the case. For example, a Home Office (2011, p 2) guidance report claims, 'domestic violence figures that relate to incidents reported in face-to-face British Crime Survey interviews should be treated with caution. Prevalence rates for domestic violence derived from the self-completion module are around five times higher for adults than those obtained from face-to-face interviews.' Furthermore, global evidence on violence against women suggests that the scale and impact of domestic violence represents an international emergency and, if understood in the same way as illness or disease, would be considered at pandemic proportions (see, for example, Ellsberg and Heise, 2005; WHO/LSHTM, 2010).

However, it has also been acknowledged that systemic or macro dynamics can and do contribute to the continuation of the *hidden* nature of domestic violence, and its silencing effects on the women who are its victims. Global evidence has shown the ways in which in almost every society across the world social institutions serve to deny, obscure and legitimise abuse. Romito (2008, p 43) argues, for example, that state tactics or strategies for hiding male violence against women are evident across the globe, and include:

Ways of seeing, conceptualising and naming reality – which materialise in behaviour, are deposited as common sense and become ideology when they centre on the interests of those in power and may be "institutionalised" in various ways, such as laws, scientific or pseudoscientific theories and the work practices of legal and social services.

Considering all of this evidence, it is perhaps easy to see why and how women victims of domestic violence are considered vulnerable in health and social care terms (as well as in respect of research ethics and governance criteria), how such susceptibility can result in serious emotional and psychological problems, as well as other physical, social and financial difficulties, and how these can result in women's loss of personal autonomy, their decision-making capacity and their ability to develop resilience (see also Moore and Miller, 1999; Humphries and Thiara, 2003; Taft, 2003). And we can perhaps also understand how these associations may be more pertinent or relevant during the victimised stage, that is, when violence or abuse is ongoing in women's lives, when they don't want, or feel unable, to report it, and when support services designed to help these women are inadequate or ineffective. It is during these times when domestic violence can contribute to women's sense of powerlessness, vulnerability and isolation (see, for example, Seeley and Plunkett, 2002).

This does not necessarily mean, however, that women victims of domestic violence are at all times passive or unresisting in their attempts to address, lessen or prevent abuse or violence in the domestic setting. Many women adopt strategies for resistance or, more commonly, for protection, and in this respect women's negotiation of personal safety and that of their children, for example, needs to be acknowledged, or at the very least seen as evidence of women's resilience or coping strategies (if not necessarily their agency) in stressful and traumatic settings (see Ellsberg and Heise, 2005; Wilcox, 2006; Williamson, 2010). However, most women also need timely and appropriate help and support in developing resilience and strategies for escaping domestic violence simply because, as Taft (2003, p 220) argues, women 'rarely take action on their own behalf', and require interventions – through formal health and social care support services, family and friends where appropriate, and criminal justice agencies – in order to recognise the abuse for what it is, understand that it is wrong, and to decide to put an end to self-blame behaviour and thinking where this occurs.

Sadly, the likelihood of women being able to access these necessary sources of support both currently and in the future are considerably reduced in the context of the current global economic crisis and the erosion of welfare state provision in countries worldwide. In the UK, there are genuine concerns that the introduction of Universal Credit, for example, will have disproportionate impacts on women victims of domestic violence and their children and, coupled with the cuts to domestic violence services, 'may result in some survivors ether returning to the violent relationship or prevent them from leaving' at all (Women's Aid, 2012, p 2). Furthermore, recent global research based on women's stories, as well as reports and case studies from unions and non-governmental organisations (NGOs) conducted by the Trades Union Congress (TUC) (2011, introduction), show the extent to which the economic crises has affected women globally, resulting in unemployment, lack of job security, and 'the increased risk of sexual and domestic abuse.'

Ethical and methodological considerations in research with victims-survivors of domestic violence

As discussed in Chapter One, from both a research governance and ethical perspective – and drawing on more recent descriptors or identifiers in health and social care policy and practice – women victims-survivors of domestic violence (along with other victims of abuse or trauma) are necessarily identified as vulnerable. In the main, this is to ensure that essential safeguards are put in place to protect them from current or further abuse or violence, and to ensure that research processes in and of themselves don't further endanger the lives of such participants (see Ellsberg and Heise, 2005; WHO/LSHTM 2010; ESRC, 2010).

Under Department of Health and ESRC research governance frameworks, research participants are also considered vulnerable if they are *likely* to be susceptible to coercion, harm or exploitation. For women victims-survivors of domestic violence there is also a *potential* high degree of further risk involved when participating in research that might result in them being subject to harm or coercion should their abuser discover they are taking part, for example (see Ellsberg and Heise, 2005). What is also particularly relevant to research with women victims-survivors of domestic violence, and victims of abuse or trauma more generally, is that research that focuses on 'sensitive topics' can also potentially create or enhance (existing) vulnerability among research participants. As has already been discussed (see Chapter One), ESRC guidance makes specific reference to participants' experiences 'of violence, abuse or exploitation' as evidence of such 'sensitivity' in research terms (2010, p 9). Reference is also made to the need for strict ethical regulation and procedures where research might result in psychological distress to participants, or might require researchers to breach confidentiality because of harm or risk disclosures – this is particularly relevant to participants who have experienced, or are experiencing, child abuse or domestic violence, for example, or where participants' children may also be at risk.

The essential safeguards needed when working with women victims of domestic violence should therefore include ensuring women's anonymity and safety throughout the research process; the use of advocates or intermediaries where necessary; ensuring a safe place for women to participate in the research process, and that their safety is a primary and ongoing concern throughout the research process and beyond; strict adherence to the safe storage of research data; and ensuring researchers have the necessary skills and expertise to work sensitively, safely and collaboratively with such women (see WHO, 2001).

A further consideration in working with women victims of domestic violence in research is the specific nature of their vulnerability or marginalisation, the causes of which are often rooted in the silencing effects of domestic violence. Thus, it is vital when planning research with these participants that careful consideration is given to the precise nature of the vulnerability (the fact that victims-survivors of domestic violence are often multiply vulnerable or marginalised) and the types of methods intended, based on flexible and individual, even case-by-case, approaches where necessary, and in consultation with participants themselves. This will mean going beyond standard ethical procedures that ensure respect for participants at all stages of the research process and maximising benefits to participants (Ellsberg and Heise, 2005), and will require specific attention to factors that minimise harm, enhance strategies for personal safety and enable researchers to negotiate successfully both the risks and benefits of research on violence and abuse.

Harvey (2011, p 665) has argued: 'researching intimate moments in participants' lives can be challenging for researchers who seek to understand hard to reach populations [or] private spheres that can pose practical and ethical problems to observe or record.' This is particularly true of research that involves vulnerable or marginalised groups such as women victims of domestic violence who are often difficult to identify, access and recruit on to research studies, in part because the silencing effects of domestic violence mean they don't necessarily report abuse in formal contexts; nor do they necessarily seek support from service providers. As Simmons and colleagues (2011, p 1229) state, 'most women in abusive/controlling relationships simply do not utilize formal helping structures (eg, shelters, domestic violence support groups, hot lines).' Thus, while we know a great deal about the prevalence and impacts of domestic violence on women as a result of evidence from research studies from across the globe that have involved women both directly and indirectly as research participants, in the main this evidence has been obtained from women who are known to, or have used, formal domestic violence services or other sources of support. In empirical terms then, we understand much less about those missed in comparison to those 'captured' in and by research (Abdul-Quader et al, 2006, p 11).

Identifying and recruiting women victims-survivors of domestic violence in research

It is commonly acknowledged that in such contexts identification, access and recruitment strategies must inevitably rely on non-probability sampling, such as convenience or snowball sampling, for example. Indeed, some have argued that peer identification and recruitment techniques are often more successful among marginalised populations than any strategies used by researchers themselves (see Platt et al, 2006; Gile and Handcock 2010).

Researchers who look to recruit multiply vulnerable or marginalised individuals also often rely on gaining access to participants at specific locations or in more visible communities, including, for example, street-based locations and emergency treatment centres (see Abdul-Quader et al, 2006; Platt et al, 2006; Rodriguez et al, 2006). However, the nature, extent and impacts of domestic violence on women mean that the abuse may not have been disclosed outside the immediate domestic sphere or the abusive relationship itself, and thus is not identified, or identifiable, in any known group or 'community'. Furthermore, abused women may also engage in self-denying behaviour, as one of the effects of the violence itself, and may also be afraid to disclose abuse for fear of putting themselves and their children at further risk. We also know that even when they are forced to present to services, for emergency medical treatment, for example, women may attempt to conceal the abuse even when it has resulted in physical injuries to themselves *or* they are never asked about it by those health professionals responsible for their treatment (see Hegarty and Taft, 2001). Thus, even tried and tested methods of identifying and recruiting other vulnerable, excluded populations for research purposes are often neither appropriate nor achievable for populations such as abused women.

In essence, what is needed when attempting to recruit and work with multiply vulnerable, unsupported women victims of domestic violence (in order to address real gaps in knowledge) is for researchers to strike the right balance between devising appropriate and sensitive ways of successfully identifying and working with these women, and in ensuring that their safety and rights are at the forefront of research design and praxis. In short, as Penrod and colleagues (2003, p 101) argue, researchers must endeavour to 'balance the acquisition of knowledge with the rights of participants.' In terms of recruitment procedures, convenience sampling would seem to be the most appropriate and effective means of identifying and gaining access to unsupported women victims of domestic violence, and often word-of-mouth approaches can work best here. In her study of women who experienced domestic violence in Calcutta, for example, Sen (1999) used word-of-mouth techniques – cold-calling in slums, contact with activists and even her friends and family in Calcutta – in order to identify and access her sample of largely hidden victimised women.

Similarly, Rodriquez and colleagues' (2006, p 87) study of Spanish-speaking Latino families in a rural community in the US found personal contacts to be the most useful method of identification and recruitment, even after multiple strategies for recruitment had been used: 'the research team learned that word of mouth and the use of existing community resources were the most powerful recruitment strategies.' In identifying unsupported victims of domestic violence, such word-of-mouth techniques are often critical, although in many respects they are much less likely to result in high numbers of women participants, and thus may necessitate small-scale qualitative methods and approaches. This does not mean, of course, that the rigour or credibility of the research is inevitably surrendered for the sake of access, but that this must be balanced against the necessity of 'conducting studies in populations where inherent barriers exist relative to key issues such as recruitment, attrition, *sampling size...*' (Crosby et al, 2010, p 1; emphasis added).

The practical and methodological challenges involved in identifying and accessing women who, by the very nature of their abusive experiences, are largely silent and hidden, also points to, and indeed, necessitates, an *intensive* rather than an extensive methodological approach. This is also particularly the case when using new, different, or exploratory participatory methods, for example, that also involve individualised narrative approaches that facilitate, and indeed, emphasise participant 'voice' (see the discussion below).

Furthermore, in common with victims of other forms of trauma such as torture, kidnapping, child abuse and so on (see Pritchard and Sainsbury, 2004), women victims of domestic violence can often be reluctant to open up or talk about their experiences even when they are identified and recruited on to studies (this was one of the main reasons for introducing different ways of facilitating 'voice' in the PNR study, of ensuring that the women's stories could be told in full and written and produced in their own space and time; see the discussion below). For example, fear of reprisal, the need to protect themselves and their children, lack of financial independence, discrimination, and concern that they won't be believed, are all highly pertinent factors when considering women's capacity and willingness to disclose and talk about their experiences of domestic violence using conventional qualitative methods (such as interviews, focus groups, and so on).

The 'silencing' effects of domestic violence are widely recognised in the literature as contributing further to women's feelings of disempowerment, isolation and fear (Dobash and Dobash, 1992; Romito, 2008; Banyard, 2010; Williamson, 2010), and, as stated, these effects occur not only as a result of the personal, psychological effects of domestic violence, but also external influences such as, for example, inadequate or inappropriate support services, poor counselling practice and the shortcomings of criminal justice agency responses. All of these issues have consequences for women's participation in research if they are not identified, approached and included in the right ways – as Ellsberg and Heise (2005, p 49) propose, women victims of domestic violence thus need to be asked about their experience in 'sympathetic, non-judgemental' ways.

These issues and challenges have, to a large extent, resulted in gaps in current research and understanding about the experiences and needs of unsupported women victims of domestic violence, and perpetuate problems of access and participation. While a number of studies in different countries have used PR and PAR (including participatory appraisal) methods when working with women victims-survivors of domestic violence, such methods are less commonly used even in studies of domestic violence that use in-depth qualitative approaches (see Ellsberg and Heise, 2005). Furthermore, the kinds of PR methods that have been used tend either to rely on conventional interview or focus group techniques or do not describe in any detail the extent (and limitations) of the participatory approach analytically, interpretively and so on. In other words, and as stated in discussions so far about the limitations of some studies that claim to be participatory, researchers do not necessarily define the parameters of PR or its methods. It is also the case that PAR and participatory appraisal methods are often used in studies that are conducted in community settings or among participant *groups* rather than with individual, vulnerable or marginalised participants.

While ownership of data and empowerment of individuals and communities through social change outcomes are among the key principles and intentions outlined specifically in domestic violence studies that use PR or PAR, it is not always clear how such objectives are possible or realised among multiply vulnerable or marginalised (and unsupported) women victims of domestic violence. The purpose and underlying principles of the PNR study (described below) were to address some of these issues and oversights, and to ensure that the voices of these unsupported women were heard using methods that emphasised authorial control and ownership of data (their own narratives/stories) as well as some degree of personal (rather than structural) transformation.

Working with women victims–survivors of domestic violence in research

Feminist perspectives and empiricism

The objectives of the PNR project with women victims–survivors of domestic violence, as in most other domestic violence research, were underpinned and informed by feminist theory and praxis. Indeed, nearly three decades of research in this field have been influenced and shaped by feminist perspectives, which, as Ulin and colleagues argue, focus 'on the political dimension inherent in understanding [constraints] from the standpoints of people in different power and gender positions' (2002, p 17). Feminist perspectives and approaches have also been hugely influential in terms of the types of interventions, support and services offered to women who have been abused, including, for example, models of domestic violence counselling practice (see Seeley and Plunkett, 2002).

Furthermore, in common with PR and PAR methods, feminist ethnography and standpoint approaches have located women centrally in research studies, including in research on violence against women (VAW), as 'legitimate sources of knowledge' (Campbell and Wasco, 2000, p 773). As Ford-Gilboe and colleagues have also stated (1995, p 17), the aim here as been to 'expose hidden power imbalances and to empower those involved to understand, as well as to transform, the world.' Of course, there can be a number of tensions between epistemology, research practice and women's personal experiences of violence, and it can sometimes be difficult for the researcher involved in working collaboratively with research participants to reconcile these tensions (see Aldridge, 2012b), especially when working with vulnerable women such as these, who often require flexible, individualised (even 'bespoke') methodological approaches. Some of these conflicts have been debated in the reflexive accounts of feminist ethnographers and historians (see, for example, Websdale, 1995; Skeggs, 2001), and it is here that, despite the claims and counter-claims about the role of reflexivity in research (see Chapter Five), these personal interjections and insights have contributed new knowledge and understanding about the importance of standpoint feminist perspectives and women's central roles in research. More than 30 years ago now Oakley (1979), for example, posited that the views and experiences of women themselves were of equal validity to that of so-called academic and research 'experts' (see also Cotterill and Letherby, 1993; Haaken, 2010).

However, the need for greater accommodation and synergy at the intersection between feminist theory, research practice and women's own experiences continues to be both pertinent and pressing. And it is perhaps here more than anywhere else that participatory approaches can accommodate and facilitate this kind of interconnectedness, particularly when these methods are based on more democratic and empathic principles and are more genuinely inclusive and collaborative. As has been discussed, in PR there is recognition of the importance of the contributions and 'voices' of participants in research, as well as understanding that such research should contribute both new knowledge and, where possible, lead to social change outcomes. What is important in terms of PR with women victims-survivors of domestic violence is that it is not just women's victimised-survivor voices that are heard, but also their *research* voices, as initiators, investigators, writers, analysts and co-analysts (see also the discussion in Chapter One).

Participatory narrative research: the Write It project

Both the concept and impetus for the PNR (Write It) project with women victims-survivors of domestic violence emerged as a result of evidence from secondary analysis of data from a two-year study of mothers who had serious and enduring mental health problems, and whose children were contributing to their informal care (see Aldridge and Becker, 2003), *and* recognition of a noted gap in evidence on research with *unsupported* women victims-survivors of domestic violence. The latter specifically pointed to the need for greater insight into the 'characteristics and dimensions' of domestic violence (Ellsberg and Heise, 2005, p 11) among those women who have not used domestic violence services.

Secondary analysis of data from the two-year study of children who lived with and cared for parents with mental illness (Aldridge and Becker, 2003) revealed that 23 out of the 35 mothers interviewed for the study had been abused and talked openly, without being asked, about their experiences of domestic violence. Many of these women also said that they believed their mental health problems had been triggered by past sexual, physical or emotional abuse. Pat, for example, described the symptoms of her obsessive compulsive disorder (OCD), which manifested themselves in obsessively checking that the windows and doors in her house were locked. She attributed this behaviour to her former partner's violence towards her and their children:

> He had my children at knifepoint … and I think maybe with my doors and things he used to come … even after he left, he used to come and kick all the windows and everything in so maybe that is where I get my OCD from. (quoted in Aldridge and Becker, 2003, p 40)

What was also notable from the secondary analysis of the mental health data was that, for the women themselves, the real reason – as they saw it – for the onset of their mental health problems was not being addressed in any therapeutic sense because their experiences of domestic violence had not been considered an aetiological factor in their diagnoses. And yet the connection between domestic violence and mental illness among women who are its victims is well documented in research across the globe (see, for example, Hughes and Jones, 2003; Taft, 2003).

Aims and objectives of the participatory narrative research project

The PNR project aimed to gain insight into women's experiences of domestic violence by taking an intensive participatory approach that would reveal, in the women's own words, the ways in which they had experienced, responded to, and survived domestic violence (from their partners or former partners) without help or intervention from formal domestic violence services. Thus, the intention was to include the narratives of women who weren't or hadn't been in receipt of domestic violence services in order to try and identify the dimensions and characteristics of abuse in relation to stress factors and resilience and survival tactics among the women participants.

However, in recognising the silencing effects of domestic violence on women, as well as the noted gaps in research evidence from unsupported (silenced) women, one of the main objectives of the study was to identify new ways of working with the victims-survivors of domestic violence in research,[3] based on more emancipatory and inclusive principles and using autobiographical, participatory writing as a specific narrative technique. In methods terms, then, the intention was to emphasise agency and 'voice', and to move away from a strictly victimised 'script' to explore what has been described as 'the DNA of personal response ... a point of refraction between external structure and personal agency' (Goodson, 2013, p 7; see also Aldridge, 2013). While in the domestic violence literature women's agentic stances in response to domestic violence have been noted (see Wilcox, 2006), I would argue that these can and should be reinforced in research methods with women participants that emphasise specifically 'top-end' inclusive and emancipatory techniques (see Chapter Six). Thus, the PNR study facilitated ownership and control of the data (by the women themselves); women's agency (choice over how they constructed their narratives and how these were analysed and presented); and opportunities for self-analysis of the data through reflexive processes.

In many respects, the intentions of the PNR project were as much methodological as they were evidential in that the focus was on understanding the efficacy of the participatory narrative method itself as well as on generating new insights and knowledge about domestic violence and its effects on unsupported women victims. Thus, the key aims and objectives of the study were to:

- illustrate the efficacy of using participatory written narrative approaches with women victims-survivors of domestic violence that emphasised both agency and 'voice';
- demonstrate the advantages and challenges of including participants as co-researchers and co-analysts in research processes;
- use written narrative approaches to address the interpretive and representational challenges involved in analysing and explicating qualitative narrative data by encouraging participants themselves to take on authorial, analytical and reflexive roles;
- consider the important ethical issues and challenges that emerge when conducting research with women victims-survivors of domestic violence;

- identify both stress and resilience factors in women's lives when they are victims of domestic violence, in particular, when they are not supported by domestic violence services.

In the main, because the study was intensive rather than extensive (that is, based on individualised accounts from a small sample of women),[4] the intention was to use the study to inform further methodological debates about participatory techniques, and highlight aspects of the women's experiences as unsupported victims of domestic violence, rather than to make broad claims or generalisations based on (small-scale) evidence.

Participatory narrative research method

The objective in the PNR project was not to recruit large numbers of women to the study, but to obtain a richness of data through small numbers of participants, allowing the women to tell their own stories of domestic violence in their own time using written narrative approaches. These were based on 'real dialogue rather than one-way communication', and a more creative or imaginative approach (Wilcox, 2006, p 729). These types of intensive approaches are, as Crosby and colleagues (2010, p 3) argue, limited in their statistical influence to test hypotheses and effects, but their value lies more in 'addressing gaps in empirical literature and evidence as these gaps may be valuable for informing public health policy and practice' (the acknowledged evidence gap here relates precisely to the fact that we know very little about the experiences of unsupported women victims of domestic violence). Furthermore, much narrative research is premised not on quantity but on quality of data from smaller sample sizes that 'results in unique and rich data that cannot be obtained from experiments, questionnaires or observations' (Crosby et al, 2010, p 3).

In many respects, the PNR project adopted similar techniques to an intensive case study approach where the researcher focuses 'on only one specific instance of the phenomenon to be studied ... each instance is studied in its own specific context, and in greater detail than in extensive research' (Swanborn, 2010, p 2; see also Benbasat et al, 1987; Plummer, 2001; Yin, 2004; Simons, 2009). The project also borrowed elements from life story research which, as Atkinson (1997, p 8) proposes, is 'the story a person chooses to tell about the life he or she has lived, told as completely and honestly as possible. What is remembered of it, and what the teller wants to know of it' (see also Lieblich et al, 1998). However, to some extent life story or life history research also implies chronology, or some linear progression in the telling or recounting of the story, and thus both in design and methods terms the way in which the data are obtained are to some extent presupposed or fixed, usually in the form of a guided interview by a researcher.

The key focus of the PNR project was to obtain evidence about women's experiences of domestic violence elicited through self-authored written narratives, but how they told that story and in what style or form was entirely up to the women themselves (this could be in diary form, first-person accounts, written as fiction, and so on). The written method was also chosen because evidence from health studies has revealed the therapeutic benefits of narrative writing for victims of abuse and trauma (see Birren and Birren, 1997; Pritchard and Sainsbury, 2004; Bolton, 1999, 2010; see also the discussion in Chapter Five); and one of the objectives in the PNR study was to use participatory methods that could also be potentially therapeutic or transformative in a personal sense (as opposed to in a broader, more generalised way) for the women involved.

What was essential, however, was that the women's stories of domestic violence related in some way or form to incidents relating to the violence or abuse they had experienced and with reference to the parameters and objectives of the PNR project itself (which were made clear to the women participants from the outset; see Aldridge, forthcoming, 2015). Furthermore, the women's personal stories would be presented as individualised 'snapshot' life histories (see Goodson, 2013) in the broader context also of existing knowledge and insight into domestic violence and its impacts on women. In this way, what we know currently from women themselves as the victims and survivors of domestic violence, and from other research – including the secondary analysis data from the mental health study – also underpin and inform the context from which the women's stories emerge and are constructed.

Informal, word-of-mouth techniques worked best in terms of identifying and recruiting women to the PNR study. Thus, the project was publicised online, at conferences, through networks of professionals, academics, activists and student bodies, with the specific intention to recruit unsupported women, in the main, through informal, word-of-mouth processes via these networks and individuals.

The women who have volunteered their accounts for the study so far (the study is ongoing) have been unsupported survivors of domestic violence,[5] that is, they have survived abusive relationships on their own, either without seeking help from formal support services, or they failed to secure adequate or effective support when they looked for it. Drawing on these mostly retrospective survivor accounts meant that safety issues were not as critical as they would have been had the women still been involved in abusive relationships while participating in the study. When working with women victims-survivors of domestic violence (and other multiply vulnerable research participants), it is the responsibility of the researcher to report any potential risks or harm to participants (and their children, where relevant), and thus breaches in confidentiality are often inevitable – and participants must be informed of this from the outset (see the discussion in Chapters One and Two), in which case, it is often more realistic and viable to adopt a retrospective approach with such participants in order to avoid exposing women to further risks through the research process itself, as long as confidentiality and anonymity are assured and maintained (and as long as research staff are sufficiently experienced and trained in working with these kinds of participants).

Of course, this kind of emancipatory approach (see Chapter Six), that requires researchers to take a step back in the research process, particularly during the data collection phase, also demands that researchers must recognise and address the potential adverse consequences for participants of engaging with methods that require recalling, revisiting and recounting past traumatic experiences. In such instances it is thus critical for researchers to ensure that participants are not only given opportunities to withdraw from participation at any point in the research process, but also to have access to appropriate sources of support from researchers themselves and/or significant others who are aware that participants are involved in the research process from the outset.

When working with research participants such as those who are in abusive relationships, that is, *during* their participation in studies, this then raises different and more immediate ethical challenges. Not least of these is that researchers have a responsibility to report abuse or risk of abuse or harm to relevant third parties, and respondents need to be informed of this in advance of their participation in studies. However, this may result in a number of outcomes, including participants choosing to withdraw from participation and/or accepting the support that is offered, thus changing their unsupported status; the latter then has implications for the objectives of the study (for example, to research marginalised, unsupported research participants). In many respects, these challenges and dilemmas are simply the inevitable consequences of working with marginalised populations (for further discussion, see Aldridge, 2012b).

The PNR project adopted, and indeed, promoted, specific emancipatory elements (see Chapter Six, Figure 6.1) that would ensure the women participants would 'own', as authors, their personal narratives/stories of domestic violence and also have control over the telling. The women could also choose whether to take part in the research as well as whether to continue to participate (or withdraw at any time), and were given choice and control over every aspect of their narratives – its form and construction, its pace and length, as well as their positions and roles as authors/analysts. The women were also assured that their finished narratives would be presented *as written*, and would not be edited, 'cherry-picked' or subject to third party interpretation or re-presentation (see Richardson, 1994) in the final (*Write It*) anthology that resulted from the PNR study[6] (Aldridge, forthcoming, 2015). This more autonomous or emancipatory approach was chosen not only on the basis of whether it would 'fit with the purposes of [the] investigation' (Ford-Gilboe et al, 1995, p 14), but also in order to ensure and promote agency and empowerment among the women participants whose lives and experiences (particularly of violence and abuse) had been influenced, and indeed, in the main, had been governed by contrary or opposing conditions and experiences.

Issues of trust and validation

A necessary first step in making contact and working with women victims-survivors of domestic violence is to build and establish relationships of trust (that also minimise risk and harm, as discussed earlier). While this was an essential prerequisite in the study, in order to ensure the women participants were able to engage willingly and comfortably with the method, as well as the objectives of the project itself, the primary intention was to take a deliberate step back in subsequent stages in the research process, while at the same time reassuring the participants that support was on hand and readily available from researchers and others should they need it. This was in order to give the women the necessary space and time for recall, writing and reflection, and asking the women to reflect on and analyse their narratives once they were completed further augmented the emancipatory objectives of the study itself. The aim here was threefold: such an approach emphasised participation and autonomy by transposing authorial and analytical roles and processes; issues and dilemmas about (third party) interpretation and representation of the data were addressed in part through the women's authorial roles and reflexive and analytical responses (see also the discussion in Chapter

Five); and issues of 'truth' and 'being believed' were also addressed by conferring on the women authority, credence and expertise as the authors of their own stories.[7]

Regarding the latter point, it is worth noting here with respect to working with individualised (participatory) narratives in research that while we should not assume that everything that is said or written in narrative or storytelling form is authentic or 'true' in any objective sense (whatever this may be), other evidence may, for example, dispute or even refute that which is gleaned from data based on personal narratives. Equally, truth testing should not be an objective of this type of research. This is especially the case where disbelief, refutation or obfuscation characterise or reflect specific ideological perspectives on, or responses to, social issues or problems, such as domestic violence (see Romito, 2008). While in some cases personal stories may not be believed or accepted as 'real' or valid by others (or at particular points in time), it must be acknowledged that they are considered authentic and real in their consequences for those who experience and live through them, and this is often of critical importance to narrators/writers themselves.

Nevertheless, even when drawing on what we know from evidence and public discourses about the nature and impact of vulnerability and victimisation, this does not always help individual stories to be validated or confirmed in certain, and often critical, contexts (and particularly for those who experience victimisation, abuse, and so on). This is particularly true of women's experiences of domestic violence. For these women there can be a pervasive and sometimes pernicious dichotomy between what, subjectively, is real to them and political, ideological and personal influences and perspectives (at both macro and micro levels) that may serve to undermine the impact of their experiences, and whether others understand or believe them. For example, while these women may carry the emotional as well as the physical scars of their violent encounters, the responses of others, for example, the police, or legal representatives and even those closest to women victims, such as relatives and friends, may serve to discredit or negate women's experiences of abuse, or fail to take them seriously (see Bancroft, 2002; Williamson, 2010; Aldridge, 2013; see also HMIC, 2014).

Thus, even though some might argue that research methods that invite and rely on the personal or subjective narratives of participants should not and cannot be considered true, accurate or, in fact, 'correct', knowing their stories or narratives will be read and understood as valid and truthful (the process of being believed) is often of critical importance for the narrators of such stories, including (and perhaps, especially) for women victims-survivors of domestic violence (this is evidenced in the reflections of all the women who took part in the PNR study; see Aldridge, 2013). Lieblich and colleagues (1998, p 2) also propose that narrative research is distinct from other methods that may search for or presuppose 'truth' precisely because of the underlying assumption that there is 'neither a single, absolute truth in human reality nor one correct reading or interpretation of texts.'

Furthermore, it is also important to acknowledge that for many people, psychological 'truth' is of equal value to factual 'truth' (see Portelli, 1998); thus, what is 'true' for participants engaged in telling their stories or narratives in PR, for example, should be treated as 'real' or valid for them personally (even though this may conflict with conventional ideas about what constitutes 'valid' evidence). With respect to the specific example of women victims-survivors of domestic violence and the PNR study, the method itself was chosen intentionally to convey to the women participants – some of whom had not told their stories before and certainly not in the form of written accounts – that their narratives were important and valid, not just in the context of the project itself, but also outside it, as accounts of worth in their own right (as stated, these accounts will be presented, as written, in a published anthology of the women's domestic violence narratives; see Aldridge, forthcoming, 2015).

The intention in the second half of this chapter is to present a specific narrative example from the PNR study in the form of Rosie's account of domestic violence written in the style of a letter to her former abusive partner.[8,9] The objective here is to demonstrate the value and weight of the participatory narrative account within a PR framework and methodology, and to demonstrate the cogency of participant 'voice' in a more immediate, 'real time', context. Rosie's autobiographical account is intentionally presented in full and unedited and in line with the original objectives of the research (and in accordance with assurances made to all of the women who took part from the outset that this would be the case), thus avoiding outcomes (and outputs) that present data as 'genuine evidence' but that are so often 'pruned and spruced up for their textual appearance' (Richardson, 1994, p 518). Issues relating to (different kinds of) narrative analyses and interpretations as well as reflexivity are discussed in Chapter Five, as well as Rosie's own reflections on and analysis of her own account.

Rosie's narrative

Dear Tom,

It's been nine years since we split up. Financial, physical, sexual, emotional abuse – that's quite a CV. I've decided I can't carry on hating you, it's not a healthy emotion to keep bottled up. I pity you now as I'm sure you've not changed in the years since I left you. I'm writing this letter to you as form of closure on the 7 years I spent with you. What shocks me about the situation I was in was how it was ignored and dismissed by friends and those people who were in a formal position to help me. If I was a child under 18, I'm sure my case of abuse would have been seen as a serious case, but because I was an adult and woman, I should have acknowledged that I need help and found those who could have helped – according to those in authority.

You don't start a relationship thinking it's going to end in violence and tears. In the beginning you seemed like the perfect boyfriend, from a 'good' family, 'good' prospect, romantic and caring. We meet at college; you were the year above me. I'd seen you about and you always seemed like a 'nice' sort of lad. We started seeing each other after being away on a college field trip in Wales. I suppose in some ways you were the opposite of the boys living on the estate where I grew up, polite and independent. Looking back I think I was in awe of your family and your family home, it was a world away from where I grew up. My parents were very loving towards each other and me – I have never seen my Dad hit my Mum. They never argued, just the odd silence.

It's really hard to say when the abuse started in our relationship, looking back there were insights in to it before we started to live together. We'd go out at the weekend and you'd drink too much and then pick fights with me for no reason. At this point it was just arguing and no violence involved. Yet it wasn't every time we went out, we had some nice weekends away and nights together. My family thought you were the ideal boyfriend for me, they were happy when we moved in together.

Our first place together was in the village where you grew up; all of your friends were in the village. I was in my final term of college, you used to drop me off and pick me up as we had one car which you needed for work. I felt so isolated in the village, only 2 buses a day came into the village, I couldn't visit my friends and family. I'd spend my time in the house on my own. Eventually, after left college I lost touch with my own group of friends. You thought they weren't a good influence on me, thinking I'd get drunk with them and leave you for someone else. Looking back on things, I think you felt threatened by me having other people in my life other than you. Your friends became my friends. For years, your friends couldn't understand why we were together. Even they thought how you spoke to me and treated me was out of order.

If you'd had a bad day at work, you'd come home and start bitching at me. Why was this a mess? You didn't like what I'd cooked for you, your favourite was telling me I was stupid and fat. I decided that I didn't want to go to university, pressure from you and you had been steadily eroding my self-confidence. People may think it's odd but I really can't remember when things became violent. I'm sure it was when I finished college and got a full time job. Normally you wouldn't hit me unless you were drunk. Yet even drunk you were cunning in where you hit me, never in the face, rather my ribs, stomach, arms, back or anywhere my clothes would cover that. I'd often invite friends back to the house after we'd been out; hoping that with them in the house would stop you being vicious or you'd pass out drunk. Friends had seen you attack me on the way home from a night out, slamming me into a fence, breaking my ribs and kicking me when I lay on the floor. It's amazing how they could turn their heads the other way. If I spoke to them about it afterwards, they would shrug and say if it was serious, I'd leave you.

Despite you always belittling me, I managed to get a good job and have a successful career. Yet you still managed to control me when I was at work. I tried to sit my professional qualifications, but you'd do anything to stop me from studying. You constantly told me I was stupid, fat, ugly and that I was lucky to have you, but you were obsessed that I was having affairs at work. You'd hide in the car park to see who I'd walk out to the car with. After being told that you're worthless and stupid you start to believe it. I must have seemed miserable but I never spoke to my parents about what was going on, they saw glimpses of how you spoke and treated me generally. They were shocked that I didn't have my own bank account and only our joint account, which I had to tell you every time I spent something. My parents didn't like the way you treated me but they thought if I was unhappy with it, I'd leave you. Another part of the process of you keeping me down was you flirting with other girls and even sleeping with them. You constantly told me that why would anyone want to have sex with someone fat and ugly like me. Again, again and again you told me I should be grateful to have man like you.

For whatever reason I put up with it, always thinking the violence would stop. Your behaviour had become the norm. After we'd been together for a couple of years, your behaviour became more and more bizarre and erratic. If I refused to argue with you, you'd bite your hand down to the tendons or head butt the door. Or you would repeat one word over and over again, this could last for a couple of hours. I think you tried to mimic the behaviour of your grandfather – you worshipped him. He treated your grandmother much the same way you treated me, I can't say about the violence but the verbal and mental abuse – yes. He believed that women were second class citizens and should be good breeders, generally their only good purpose in life.

By the time we'd moved into our second house, your attacks on me wouldn't just be when you were drunk, but mainly drink fuelled the worst of them. One Saturday morning I'd put marmalade on your toast and you wanted jam, so in a rage you threw the plate in my face, chipping a tooth. I think you'd come to realise that you had a power over me because your behaviour was unpredictable with no pattern to the abuse. I'd be sitting watching TV and you'd walk over to me and give me a hug, while you'd stub your cigarette out on my hand, I have to look at my scarred hands everyday. Another of your favourites was to stick out your foot and trip me up as I walked by. Generally, when you hit me, you'd still make sure the bruises couldn't be seen by anyone. I never knew bruises could last for 6 weeks, bruising seemed sometimes to go right down to my bones.

I never thought when you were hitting me that I deserved it, but I didn't know what to do about it. I prayed that someone would notice and they'd help me. But looking back how anyone would help me if I didn't tell anyone what was happening. You'd told me that if I left you that you would kill me. One a good day, you'd only promise to leave me with nothing.

You decided that we'd get married; you told everyone that I'd accepted and I didn't dare not to agree to marry you. We would go a couple of months without you really physically hurting me, minor smacks, but the mental and financial abuse never let up, this was just part of my life now. I wasn't excited like a girl getting married should be; I was just resigned to it happening. Your mum took over the wedding planning, she had the perfect day. One reason I think I let your Mum take over the wedding, was that your sister was mentally handicapped and she'd never get married. Friends I worked with asked me over and over if I was making the right decision, I must have seemed as if I wasn't sure about it, but I just let the day carry on. Even on my hen night, which was a quiet meal with our families and a few of my 'approved' work friends, you came back home ranting and smashing up the house, because you were certain I'd got a man in the house. There was no man in the house, I'd never been unfaithful to you.

One of your most vicious attacks on me was on the Christmas Eve after we'd got married, I'd got gastric flu and had asked you to stay home with me as I felt so poorly. You refused as you were out with your mates and accused me of trying to ruin your night out. I ended up having to ring your parents to fetch you out of the pub. So for ruining your night out with the boys you punched my stomach until I passed out.

A few months later when I found out I was pregnant, you screamed I'd done it to keep you. I was so upset about bringing a baby into our relationship. You pushed me down the stairs and kicked me in the stomach, I miscarried and because of the damage I can't have children. You used your 'upset' over my miscarriage to explain to your parents why you had written off their car because you were drunk. They said it was understandable.

You had started to become a lot less choosey where you hit me, I got more and more black eyes, or split lips. I had to take time off from work on the sick, how could I go to work and explain the state of my face. I lied to my parents, even arguing with them so I didn't visit them for a week or more.

I felt like I was living a double life, confident and strong at work and at home a beaten and miserable person, who would believe me? That was my fear, being believed, being pitied or worse still being thought of as stupid. It got to the point where I had to leave my job, I just couldn't explain my absences any more, and I thought I had no choice. So your Dad offered me a job working in the 'family' business. I think your parent's behaviour has impacted on how you are as adult. I witnessed your mum punch your dad in the face, blacking his eye. Saying that, your dad thought it was acceptable to hit me round the head if I did something he didn't like. You'd told me that your dad used to hit you when you were younger and that your parents would get drunk and hit each other when they argued. I'm not excusing your behaviour towards me but it must be a factor.

Working for your parents, I'd become even more trapped, I'd lost the tiny bit of independence I had. If I didn't go into work for a few days, you told them I was having one of my 'moments', you managed to convince them that I was mentally unstable, ill and that I was suffering from depression. It was a nice cover story for you.

We'd gone out one night and you attacked me with a piece of wood, hitting me in the face, all over. I must have been screaming loudly as remember laying on the floor with you shouting and swearing at me, when the police turned up, someone had called them because of me screaming. They shone their torches in my face, spoke to you and not me, asking if everything was ok. You said I'd fallen over drunk and smacked my face on the floor. I was so scared, in shock and pain that I didn't say anything. They said I should be more careful and shouldn't drink so much. If they'd bothered to kneel down and talk to me they would have realised I wasn't drunk, I'd not drank for months and that there was a bloody bit of wood next to me. They looked relieved when you pulled me up and said you'd get me home. Maybe they did realise what was going on, and they didn't want to get involved in another domestic case. Or maybe I should have been brave enough to speak up for myself and tell them what you had done to me. I had to have three weeks off from work, you told your parents, and I was depressed and couldn't work. I felt that I had lost total control over my life.

It was through meeting one of your old school friends, that made me realise there might something better in life than you and that I deserved to be happy. He'd not had to get used to how you treated me, like all your other friends had. He was shocked how you spoke to me, he couldn't understand why I'd stand by and let you humiliate me. He started to talk to me about how he and his family were treated by his dad, he knew the signs of abuse. He talked to me about how his Mum coped and found the strength to leave his dad. There was never anything in this relationship other than friendship. When I left you, you automatically assumed I was leaving you for him. In fact we never started to see each other until 6 months after I left you. But the fact I wasn't divorced from you, I still felt like I was having and an affair – your friends, would call me a slut and a slag when they saw me out didn't help with this. It's only in the last two or three years that I am confident to go into the town on my own without panicking that I am going to see you, your family or your friends. I know I have done nothing wrong or anything to be ashamed of.

Towards the last 6 months of our marriage, I found the courage to start standing up to you. One of the main reasons, was we got a puppy, I saw how you treated a defenseless animal and it made me so angry. I'm certain that you were jealous of my attention being directed at her, you'd beat her with a brush handle if she made a mess, and you split her nose open once. You then started talking about us trying for children through IVF, this was another thing you could hurt me with, you said it was my fault we couldn't have children. I was appalled at the thought of this, I saw how you treated a puppy, what would you have been like around a baby? I decided that I had to leave you somehow, but I had no idea how or when. So I started to put some money aside, a leaving/divorce account. I couldn't have the statements arrive at our home, so I had them sent to my mum's address. As you accounted for every penny that I spent, I would ask for £10 or £20 pounds cash back with the weekly food shop. I decided that I couldn't cope any longer, I'd started to think about killing myself. One reason I felt like this was I couldn't bear you near me, I didn't want to have sex with you at all, I'd do anything to make sure I was in bed before you. Yet this didn't stop you raping me when you were drunk. I didn't realise it was rape at the time, how could it be, we were married. I only found out a few years ago that a wife can be raped by her husband.

But I realised I couldn't kill myself, I knew how much I loved my family and I couldn't put them through that. I didn't know how to tell them about what had been happening. My chance came when I went shopping with my mum, I wanted to try some clothes on and it was a big changing room so mum came in with me. As I got changed she saw the bruises and scratches on my body. When we talked about what had happened, I never realised the impact on my parents, they felt guilty and ashamed because they thought they had let me down. They were upset that I felt I couldn't talk to them about what had been happening. They knew about the verbal and financial abuse but they thought if I was in serious harm that I would have gone to them to talk about it.

Around the same time you had broken your leg and nearly had to have it amputated because of complications, my mum urged me to leave you, yet I felt a sense of I suppose duty, that you needed me to help you. Something clicked inside me when I saw you laying there in pain, I felt more in control of my life, that you couldn't hurt me physically because you weren't capable. I realised I didn't love you, and that I couldn't remember when I did. I had been through hell living with and I didn't want to spend the rest of my life with you. Before you had broken your leg, the violence was becoming more and more serious and I thought that you would eventually kill me.

With the help of my parents, I found a divorce solicitor, who was the most amazing woman. I drafted my divorce papers with her, 12 pages of why our marriage was irreconcilable, I left them with her until I was ready and able to leave you.

I needed to get a place of my ready to move into before I felt I could leave you, which took 5 months. I moved out of our bedroom and into the spare room. At that point you told your parents that I was having a breakdown and that you thought I was going to leave. So they started interfering in what went on the house. One night your mum came to the house threatening me that if I didn't move back into the same room as you and give you the proper care that you needed while your leg healed she would throw me out of my own house. In the argument that followed I told her exactly what sort of person her son was and why I had moved out of the bedroom. Her reaction was to say that I must have deserved being hit and that I shouldn't push your buttons! I don't know what I expected from her, given that I'd seen her and your dad hit each other. She then tried to persuade me that if I left you I'd be giving up a big house, new cars, holidays and I'd be back at home living with my parents. I told her I'd rather live in a box than be with you for any longer, your mum then squared up to me and told me she'd knock the shit out me, at this point I threw her out. When I went to work, your dad smacked me across the face and told me to stop being a spoilt bitch and that it was obvious I was mentally unstable.

I wanted to leave so often in those months, but I was scared what you would do to me. I actually went to see the doctor and told him what had been happening to me, he said he had wondered as he's seen the letters from my visits to A&E but as I was a 'clever girl' he thought I'd deal with the situation. But in the end he was great, he signed me off from work until I eventually did leave you. The one thing I was really unhappy about was that he wanted me to go on anti-depressants and that they'd help me. They may be a necessary help for other people, but it was the sort help that I didn't want. I never got help from anybody like Women's Aid, I didn't want to be labelled as a victim, I also thought there would be women there experiencing far worse than me and that I shouldn't be there.

Once you were off of your crutches you became more vicious than ever. You came into my room one night, I woke up with you sat on my chest, screaming in my face and threatening to cave my head in with a hammer. I think you behaved like this because you could see that it didn't matter what you did to me, your control was slipping. You kicked the bathroom door off, when I was in there, came over to the bath and urinated over me and then walked out. Your drinking became really bad, you'd been going out 7 nights a week for a long time, but the quantity and type of drink you were having changed. You'd drink a bottle of port or wine before you went out into town, where you'd have at least 10 or 12 pints plus spirits.

To be honest, in the last few weeks we were together, it is a blur. I can't remember specific attacks, they merge into one. I had lost nearly 4 stone in weight, I couldn't eat without being sick. I was constantly on edge,

118

knowing that I had to leave you soon before you killed me. The house that I was moving into was nearly ready. I'd psyched myself up to leaving when it was. I'd been taken personal possessions, things you wouldn't notice to my mum's for weeks. I used to go when you went out and be back before you came home.

When I did leave you it wasn't planned it just happened. We had had a massive argument and a serious physical assault let me hospitalised and that was the last straw for me. You lay on the floor crying and screaming that you didn't mean to hurt me and that I couldn't leave you. You knew at that point, it was the end. I rang my parents and asked them to come over and take me to the hospital. You left, you were terrified of what they would do and say to you. When you left I went around and locked all of the doors and made sure you couldn't get back in the house. I sat waiting for my parents to turn up, you'd obviously gone to your parent's house, as a few minutes later they turned up at the house, kicking the doors and screaming for me to get out of the house. Fortunately my parents turned up, my dad was really controlled and asked them to leave before he called the police. Your mum then blocked the drive so we couldn't get to the hospital, she ripped open the door, demanded that my parents follow her back to her house, where this would be sorted once and for all. She said to my parents that I was sick and had been for a long time. The rest I can't remember, I was passing in out of consciousness.

When I got back from the hospital there was a note waiting from me from you, telling me you had gone to stay with your aunt in Holland. Mum and dad took control and arranged for 6 or 7 of their friends to come over and help me to move out. I had my things all over the county until I moved into my own place. I stayed with my mum and dad until I could move into the house. Within a week of moving out, I'd started divorce proceedings, changed my name back to my maiden name and never looked back.

I'd be lying if I said those 7 years hasn't and still does affect me now. I have panic attacks, I feel I have to be in control of everything, if I can't control something I panic. This has got better over time but they still do happen. I still have very little self esteem and I'm overly critical of anything I do or achieve. But I'm very proud of the fact that I went to Uni and gained a 1st class honours and I'm now going on to complete a PhD. I can honestly say it is only because my husband has encouraged and supported me from the minute I decided to go. He has never criticised or hurt me in anyway. He was a victim of domestic violence as child so he knows what it is like to live in a state of fear.

I know that you remarried a much younger woman than yourself, and have had children, I hope that you do not treat them in the same way that you have treated me. One of the last things you said to me before our divorce came through was that you hoped when I grew up that I'd want to be your wife again. Well I can truly say I never want to be grown up if that's the case. I still don't like to be described as a victim of domestic violence; I prefer to think of it more in terms of surviving years of abuse. I think domestic violence needs to be as socially unacceptable as child abuse before the majority people in this country take the issue seriously. Too long people have ignored what has been happening to their family, friends and neighbours, because I think domestic violence is still thought to be a private matter and not cause for public concern.

FIVE

Participatory research: interpretation, representation and transformation

Introduction

> Writing is an everyday communicative practice, which
> pervades our lives at an individual as well a societal level.
> Given the omnipresence of the written word, research into
> the role of written language in everyday communication is
> at the heart of understanding contemporary forms of social
> interaction, between institutions and communities as well
> as between individuals. (Barton and Papen, 2010, p 3)

From the perspective of contemporary anthropology, authors such
as Barton and Papen have recognised the emergence of writing as a
cultural practice in which, importantly from a participatory standpoint,
authors and autobiographers are seen as valued contributors in their
own right, rather than simply as subjects of study distinct from
the 'professional' researcher/analyst. Furthermore, contemporary
anthropological investigations have also focused on the social and
political contexts in which written texts are produced. Indeed, the
authors argue that the examination of written works is imperative in
order to understand the structures and organisations of societies, as well
as 'how individuals and social groups organise their lives and *make sense*
of their experiences' (Barton and Papen, 2010, p 5; emphasis added).

These ideas and perspectives are congruent with the principles and
aims of the PNR study described in Chapter Four and, more broadly,
with the range of PR projects described and discussed in this book.
Thus, the same opportunities that Barton and Papen describe with
respect to written narratives from an anthropological perspective – for
facilitating 'sense-making' at an individual level and for understanding
broader social and political structures and settings – also present
themselves in many other kinds of research that use methods to
facilitate and promote participation, emancipation and 'voice', and
where research participants are more directly and actively involved in

producing research stories themselves. When considering life story research, for example, Goodson (2013, p i) proposes that the practice of storytelling is a 'crucial ingredient in what makes us human.' In this sense, we can see the importance and value of giving the participants in (qualitative) research the opportunities to present their stories or narratives in their own ways, including in written form, as well as in other creative forms such as, for example, visual, oral and textual-visual, thus in ways that confer ownership and control over the methods, form and context of narrative production.

This chapter focuses on processes of analysis and interpretation in PR, first drawing on the narrative example from the PNR study discussed in Chapter Four – Rosie's narrative specifically – in order to demonstrate some of the ways in which different kinds of narrative analyses may be conducted (both from a participant and third-party perspective). These same approaches to analysing (and co-analysing) and reading data are also relevant to PR more broadly. While there is a need to promote greater clarity and rigour with respect to PR methods, this is not to suggest that there should be a more formulaic or rule-driven method of analysing data that are generated from studies that are purposefully and necessarily varied, individualised or 'bespoke'. Rather, what PR demands is that participants should be engaged actively in the various processes of research (if that is what they want, and they are willing and able to take on a more collaborative role), including during the analytical and interpretive stages. Such an approach in PR studies also allows academic researchers to address and overcome issues of representation and to promote transformative outcomes by recognising the need, not just to equalise research roles and responsibilities, but to transpose them. Thus, transformation in PR should not just focus on the outcomes from the research itself (and the efficacy of the research methods used), but should also facilitate transformative research relationships.

Analysing and interpreting participatory data

Conventionally, the responsibility for analysing and interpreting research data falls on the academic researcher. In life history and narrative research, for example, individual stories are recalled, retold and later subject to a range of analytical processes undertaken by the academic researcher that can vary according to the methodological design and objectives of individual projects and the intentions of researchers themselves. Methods of narrative analysis can include, for example, third-party content, discourse, thematic, and even line-by-line analysis of texts (see, for example, Mishler, 1991; Fraser, 2004). This is also true with respect to many other kinds of data that are produced from qualitative studies. However, in PR, and particularly that located at the emancipatory level (see Chapter Six, Figure 6.1), analytical roles are either collaborative or self-organised, that is, they are adopted and undertaken by participants themselves or in partnership with academic researchers.

While it is most often the case in research that a degree of 'objectivity' is required in analysing data through the intervention of a third-party academic researcher, as well as analytical expertise, there is nothing to suggest that participants cannot also engage in these research processes or be trained to undertake them (see the discussion in Chapter Two and also NCAS, 2013). However, it is also the case that certain analytical techniques offer a more flexible, as well as intuitive, approach to understanding and 'reading' research data that may facilitate collaboration or much closer working relationships in research, and they can also promote independent reflections and assessments of data by participants themselves.

Taking the PNR study as an example here, the aim of giving the women participants opportunities for writing and producing their stories in full was to emphasise the value of the written (autobiographical) approach as a more emancipatory way of working. But it was also intended purposefully to avoid producing the type of transcript (based on recordings of oral interviews, for example) that was simply a 'static product' (Lieblich et al, 1998, p 8). Thus, the intention was to shift from an inert to a more fluid and immediate narrative or storytelling method – to provide a more direct entry into the lived experience of the participant-as-narrator – *and* to involve the women participants in analytical and reflexive processes in the further stages of the research process itself.

Such an approach is not unique or even new, but it is not a technique that is commonly used in qualitative research, even where personal autobiographical accounts are adopted in qualitative research studies this does not necessarily mean that the form the autobiography takes is as written text, or first-person authored account. As Plummer (2001, p 20) acknowledges, even in long life histories, the approach is often for the researcher to guide participants in writing down 'episodes' or tape-recording them for later analysis by an academic researcher (see also Atkinson et al, 1997). The objective in the PNR study was to purposefully avoid the need for sole reliance on third-party interpretation, or 'amanuensis' (Booth, 1996), in underlining and promoting a more emancipatory approach to PR.

The PNR method also facilitated a multi-dimensional approach to analysing and interpreting the data produced by the women participants, as authors. First and foremost, it allowed for the women to analyse and reflect on the data they produced (and the PNR method itself). It also enabled the reader, on first reading of the narratives in full (in this book and also in the forthcoming anthology; see Aldridge, forthcoming 2015), to make their own interpretations of the texts in the absence of any third-party 'explanations' or analyses; and it allowed for a more flexible approach to third-party 'readings' of the narratives. With respect to the latter, Lieblich and colleagues (1998, p 13) recognise the different approaches to analysing or 'reading' narrative data: 'some [narrative] *readings* ignore the context of the life story and refer to its form, the structure of the plot, the sequencing of events, its relation to the time axis, its complexity and coherence, the feelings evoked by the story, the style of narrative, the choice of metaphors or words ...' (emphasis added). The authors themselves suggest four modes of analysing or 'reading' narrative data as *holistic-content*, *categorical-content*, *holistic-form* and *categorical-form*, which incorporate a range of intrinsic and extrinsic dimensions and characteristics (of narrative form and content, plot, structure, and so on, as well as context; see Lieblich et al, 1998).

In many respects – and helpfully, in PR terms – a strictly formulaic approach to narrative research analysis and interpretation is purposefully avoided. Describing her own approach in the context of social work narratives, for example, Fraser (2004, p 186) rejects analyses and interpretations that are governed by strict 'formulas or recipes' in favour of a multi-stage consideration of the story as a whole and as a particular form or construct. This kind of approach includes various stages of analytical examination that are, to some extent, both abstract and intuitive as well as particular. We may consider the distinction between analysis and interpretation here as one that demands an examination of the data product and constitution (through some kind of coding, thematising process) in the former, and the sense- or meaning-making process that lies (perhaps more intuitively) in the latter.

For Fraser (2004), the process of analysing or 'reading' texts involves researchers listening to participants' stories and 'experiencing their emotions', note-taking and observing (and in many instances replaying) the start, unfolding and resolution of stories, followed by the transcription of narrative data and examining the specifics line by line – including identifying the kinds of stories told, their directions and any contradictions therein. This kind of approach may also involve researchers deciphering stories, 'by looking for where each line might be seen to begin and end', which could include numbering each line and 'naming' stories, while at the same time scanning 'for different domains of experience' (Fraser, 2004, p 191). Obviously, in research that involves participatory methods where participants write their own stories, line-by-line analyses and readings will be greatly facilitated.

There are also internal and external dimensions to this kind of approach, which mirrors similar approaches in other types of PR such as participatory visual methods where some form of content analysis ('counting' themes, for example) is also possible, and sometimes necessary (see Banks, 1995; see also Chapter Two). In the participatory photographic projects described in Chapters Two and Three, for example, thematic content analyses (external dimension) of the photographic data were conducted on the datasets alongside analyses conducted by participants themselves (the internal dimension). The approach adopted in the young carer mental health study involved analysing and 'reading' the visual narratives produced during the photographic diary phase:

> The narrative appraisal and content analysis were separate exercises in the research framework but not mutually exclusive phases in the research process. The content analysis … involved a systematic analysis of all forms of content and was broken down into distinct categories relating to the central aims of the study (exploring children's caring experiences and relationships in the context of parental mental ill health and gauging the efficacy of the method). (Aldridge and Sharpe, 2007, p 7)

A content analysis of the photographic data produced in the STH study (described in Chapter Three; see also Sempik et al, 2005) was also conducted in order to identify thematic patterns across the range of data produced. However, in each case (both the young carer and the STH studies) the content analyses conducted by the academic researchers were not considered more useful, valid or accurate, nor were these prioritised over the analyses and interpretations of the participants themselves.

Identifying and quantifying the content of qualitative data thematically can be useful in the context of multi-methods studies and in projects where large datasets are produced, and which allow for a multi-dimensional analytical approach (thus for both participant-researchers and academic researchers to engage in analyses either together or separately). For Fraser, for example, analysing and interpreting trauma narratives involves looking for common metaphors such as "'the aftermath", the "recovery" and "rebuilding'" (2004, p 193), and then comparisons are made *across* the range of narrative data (what I have referred to as the 'collectivising' of individual narratives; see Chapter One), looking for similarities or patterns in and across findings.

In his discussion of analysing and reading narratives in social work, Baldwin (2013, p 85) refers to the ways in which narratives can be used to 'cast new understandings of social work practice', and considers plot, trajectory, characterisation and rhetoric as elements of analysis (through the specific use of case study examples of child abuse, mental illness and disability). He does not consider narrative as only therapeutic or insightful in experiential terms for service users, but as a distinct activity that requires analysis of discourse, form, construct, language, and so on. He asserts:

> Storytelling may be a ubiquitous practice, but it is not necessarily a simple one. The material construction of the story involving emplotment, character development, scene placement and such features that are recognisable to most people reveals only part of a complex process ... power influences what and how stories are told, as well as who listens to them. This also means that while some stories are celebrated and welcomed, others are deliberately discouraged from being told, with negative consequences for those whose stories are shut down. (Baldwin, 2013, p 105)

In considering these approaches, both in terms of the generalities and the specifics of narrative analytical methods such as those described by Fraser and Baldwin, we may begin to wonder how different these approaches are from other methods of qualitative data analysis and interpretation (in effect, the 'data-processing' narrative). Thematising, coding and even counting are, after all, present in most processes of research data management and the subsequent procedures that involve telling the 'story' of the data. In PR methods, however, not only are participants involved as data producers, analysts and so on, but power influences with respect to *who* tells the story of the data, as well as *why* and *how* stories are told, are considerations that are deemed as important as the content of those stories (an issue to be discussed later in this chapter).

For example, photographic data (that produce visual stories or narratives) which are generated from studies such as the photographic participation projects described in Chapters Two and Three may be subject to thematic and content analyses as well as consideration given to the form and construction of the photographs, the location, scene, and so on. Equally important, however, from a participatory perspective, are power issues that see participant-researchers as photographers, analysts (to a lesser or greater degree) and also as subjects *in* the data. Thus, where and why participants choose to locate themselves in the photographic participation process, either as photographers and/or as subjects in the photographs themselves (that is, photographed by someone else), are also important considerations when examining visual data of these kinds, the efficacy of the method itself and the roles and positioning of the participants in the data and research processes.

The different ways of, and opportunities for, conducting *third-party* analyses of narrative data, whether in the form of written texts, visual images, and so on, are perhaps best illustrated by using Rosie's participatory narrative as an example from the PNR study, and by 'reading' or assessing it using the kinds of analytical procedures that are described and discussed above. In doing so, it is possible to demonstrate some of the ways in which third-party analyses *may* be conducted rather than showing precisely how this *should* be done (it is important to note that the analyst here could, of course, be the research participant). Furthermore, in analysing Rosie's narrative with respect to content, form and context, for example, we can demonstrate some of the different strategies for 'making sense' of the narrative, in the same way other forms of narrative might also be assessed and examined by (third-party) researchers. It should be noted, however, that the different analytical dimensions presented below – with a number of accompanying illustrative examples included – are not strictly distinct items, nor are they exhaustive, and they also demonstrate some degree of crossover or inter-sectionality.

The analytical exercise below simply demonstrates the ways in which a researcher could begin to 'read', analyse and interpret narrative data, and how these kinds of 'readings' may be transferrable in other narrative contexts, in visual or visual-textual research, for example, and also in PR studies, where research participants are actively involved as, for example, data collectors and co-analysts, depending on the nature and extent of the participatory approach (see Chapter Six for further discussion and also Figure 6.1).

Reading and analysing Rosie's (PNR) narrative

Analysis of content

Domains of experience:

- Episodes of abuse; perpetration; victimisation; resistance (and strategies for resistance/prevention: 'I'd often invite friends back to the house...'); expectation ('always thinking the violence would stop'); aftermath; survival ('I prefer to think of it more in terms of surviving years of abuse').
- Impact of these experiences: trauma – physical (bodily injuries: 'you threw the plate in my face, chipping a tooth'; 'you'd stub your cigarette out on my hand'); emotional, psychological (panic attacks; low self-esteem; fear of not being believed: 'who would believe me?'); silence.
- Recovery – emotional (courage, pride: 'I'm very proud of the fact that I went to Uni'); practical (outside help, support from others: 'my husband has encouraged and supported me ...').

Analysis of form

- Narrative style: first person, letter; tense usage; sentence structure (note the shorter, clipped sentences as Rosie describes preparing to leave Tom); plot and trajectory (how the story unfolds; linking the unfolding of the story to episodes of escalating violence); use of rhetorical questions ('who would believe me?').
- Scene placement (the location of particular episodes of violence, for example, the hospital, scenes at and outside Rosie's house).
- Characterisation: Rosie herself (as victim, survivor, daughter, partner, service user, friend of others); Tom (as partner, perpetrator, abuser, son, friend of others); others (family members, friends, close friend and new partner, professionals, pet).

Positioning (of narrator): context

- Rosie's position as writer/narrator: as letter writer, recorder of events, storyteller.
- Rosie's role as writer/narrator: recalling; reflecting: hypothesising/speculating ('if I was a child under 18'); need for reparation; self-assessment ('it's not a healthy emotion to keep bottled up'); setting the record straight; positioning in relation to others in the story

('I must have seemed miserable but I never spoke to my parents
... the saw glimpses ... they were shocked'), and the unfolding of
the story; hindsight ('looking back I think I was in awe of your
family'); comparability ('normally you wouldn't hit me unless you
were drunk').

It is clear from the above examples of the different analytical dimensions
that could be introduced when examining and assessing Rosie's
narrative, that there are some crossovers between and across these
various dimensions, as has been suggested, for example, between
'domains of experience' and 'positioning'. A specific example here
would be between the items of 'expectation' (domain of experience)
and both 'hindsight' and 'comparability' (positioning) with respect to
Rosie writing that she was 'always thinking the violence would stop'.
This is both a statement that reveals her response to the episodes of
abuse (she believed it would come to an end) and evidence of her
positioning herself as a victim/survivor in the story itself, and as a
narrator who is assessing her own story with the benefit of hindsight.
Thus she considers and places herself in the story as a victim of abuse
who believed something then (*in time*) but, with the benefit of hindsight
(as a survivor), and with the passage *of time*, recognises (now) the futility
of such a strategy.

What is also notable when considering the various analytical
dimensions above is that certain elements can be more readily subject
to third-party analysis than others. Some elements of the narrative
therefore generate clear analytical indicators, in content and form,
for example. Considering the *form* of the narrative, it is clear that it
is written as a letter, and we can see how the story unfolds based on
Rosie's experiences of abuse from her former partner Tom (*content*).
We can also clearly denote form and structural indicators such as tense
changes, the use of rhetorical questions, language, characterisation,
and so on. However, other dimensions are less obvious, and in studies
that use conventional analytical methods, further consideration by the
(third-party) analyst would be needed in order to interpret certain
aspects of the narrative such as 'positioning'.

While it is not in question that Rosie positions herself as first-person
narrator in this narrative example, the question as to *why* she chose
such an approach (as *letter* writer, for example; note Baldwin's point
here about power influences and which stories are told and how –
2013, p 105), we cannot know the answer to this for sure unless she
states this specifically in the text. In this case Rosie chooses to do so
from the outset as she engages in the process of self-reflection within

the narrative (letter) itself – 'I am writing this letter to you as a form of closure….' If she hadn't chosen to explain her choice or intention at that point, then without input from Rosie herself, the (third-party) researcher/analyst would have to make assumptions or interpretations that may not be entirely faithful, either to Rosie's experiences as a victim-survivor of domestic violence, or to her intentions as letter writer and data producer.

In the PNR study, as stated, participants were asked to consider and reflect on their narrative style and choices as well as on the finished narrative itself as part of the participatory process (this approach is also mirrored in the young carer and STH studies described in Chapters Two and Three). Such an approach was informed by an intention not to speak on behalf of participants or to make assumptions about their narrative choices and their intentions with respect to participating in the study, and thus to avoid the risk of misinterpreting their experiences and their stories (as narratives in their own right and as research data). This is just one example of the ways in which the issue of representation can be more readily addressed in PR.

In research studies that use more conventional approaches to analysing data in narrative or textual form, even when it is based on a more loosely governed or less formulaic approach to 'reading' texts, there is still a requirement on the part of the third-party analyst to interpret the data and present some form of findings discourse (which in itself is its own narrative). In the PNR study, and in the other participatory studies described in Chapters Two and Three, as well as in PR generally, the intention is not to rely solely (or indeed at all, in some cases; see the discussion in Chapter Three) on third-party analysis and interpretation, but to engage participants in collaborative and even emancipatory relationships during these processes. From a participatory perspective, it is only by involving participants at this level that the process of 'making sense' of the data can be fully realised.

Again, taking Rosie's narrative in the PNR study as an example here, we gain greater insight into the 'reading' of the story and its meaning by involving Rosie *directly* in the analytical process. From a participatory perspective, without Rosie's input, not only as author of the full account, but also as analyst and interpreter, there is a danger in misrepresenting her experiences and, in this case, in denying the potential therapeutic benefits involved (for Rosie herself) in producing, reflecting on/analysing and publishing her story in full. Thus, in the second stage of the PNR process, Rosie was invited to reflect and comment on the method itself – on the process of telling and writing her own story – as well as to engage in a degree of thematic analysis of the finished narrative (all the women who have taken part in the study so far were given the same opportunities for collaboration). This approach, again, is mirrored in that adopted in the photographic studies described in Chapters Two and Three and indeed, all of these studies demonstrate the value of a multi-dimensional approach to analysis and interpretation in PR.

With respect to the first of these reflexive strategies – the use of the PNR method itself – during the second phase of the study, Rosie reflected on and described the advantages and some of the challenges in the PNR approach, as well as commented on the reasons behind her choice of narrative style (in the form of the letter to her former partner, Tom):

> I found the method of research of benefit to me. I was able to write about my experiences in my own manner. Writing the narrative was free flowing, I did not have to stop and think about what an interviewer meant by their questions or whether what I was telling them was what they actually wanted to hear. I felt that I didn't have to justify my actions and reactions to the domestic violence I suffered. I feel it is a very non-judgemental, non-intrusive method of collecting sensitive data from participants. The only disadvantage I found with this method of data collection was it was at times very difficult writing the narrative and ensuring it would make sense to the reader. I choose to write my narrative in the form of a letter to my ex-husband. I decided upon this style of narrative as I felt it would help me achieve some closure on my experiences.

What was notable from Rosie's subsequent consideration of and reflections on her narrative from an analytical perspective was that the key themes she identified herself were wholly negative:

> I think that the key themes of my narrative are: Fear – of my husband, of me not being believed, to leave; lack of control; shame; sense of worthlessness; lack of self-esteem and confidence; isolation – from family and friends; male power and control; abuse, physical, mental, financial and sexual; unpredictability; leading a dual life – home and work; lack of support from friends, agencies such medical and police.

We can see from Rosie's thematic assessment here the importance and value of asking participants themselves to engage in reflexive and analytical processes, not necessarily (or just) because their accounts may differ from a third-party analysis, but because other considerations and pressures may be brought to bear on academic researchers from both within and outside the academy (pressure from funders, from policy makers who have different agendas, and so on; see Aldridge, 2012b), to consider or look for outcomes from research findings that simply aren't there. It is worth noting here that this was a pertinent issue in the early research on young carers, as described in Chapter Two. When these children's experiences and needs were first brought to public and political attention through the small-scale qualitative investigations undertaken by myself and colleagues in the Young Carers Research Group, for example, while the initial response (from government and from health and social care professionals) was positive – it was recognised that something must be done to help these children – equally, as researchers, we were pressed to consider and identify the positive aspects for children of caring. However, as was certainly evidenced from the early young carer studies, it was clear that these children were simply not telling us about the positive aspects of providing care for their sick or disabled parents because their experiences as the sole (unsupported, unrecognised) providers of informal care were not happy or positive ones.

In many respects, for young carers at that time it was critical that the findings from these early studies were based entirely on what the children themselves were telling us – issues that they considered to be most important in their lives – because without this, the subsequent important changes to government policy, and in health, social care and education practice, would not have taken place. Such changes have helped to transform the lives of numerous young carers and their families across the UK.

Therefore, without input from participants themselves in research that encourages and promotes their participation, collaboration, their views and distinct voices (including their reflexive and analytical voices), there is a very real danger that a different story might be presented from the one originally told. When participants are vulnerable or marginalised, it is even more vital that their views are sought and presented (and represented) fairly and faithfully, especially because these groups are more likely either to be overlooked in (conventional) research or to be included in ways that are inappropriate or ineffective.

In the PNR study, as stated, the women participants were invited to reflect on and analyse their stories in their own ways as part of the participatory process, and thus the women described the main aspects or key themes in their narratives that were notable and important to them (see Aldridge, forthcoming, 2015). In Rosie's case, the most significant aspects of her experiences as described in her own written narrative were those that had the greatest impact on her life as an unsupported victim of domestic violence (see above), and these also correspond with much of the evidence we have to date on the impacts of domestic violence on women before they seek help, as well as the fact that unsupported women victims of domestic violence are often among the most vulnerable.

Rosie was also invited to read and reflect on her narrative account at a later stage, prior to the draft typescript being submitted to Policy Press. She was also given the same opportunities for proof reading and editing that any author would have (and the same is true for all participants who are contributing to the published anthology). Commenting on this stage, Rosie wrote:

> I only made minor adjustments to my account, such as spelling and grammar. I also reworded/phrased one or two sentences. Some of the sentences had words missing from them. Also, because I found the writing process very free flowing, sometimes the sentences made sense to me but on reading them later, they seemed jumbled and confused.

All of these stages in the PNR process were important in that they demonstrated the value of collaboration and in giving participants greater access to (and equality in) writing and publishing processes. However, perhaps more importantly, the PNR project reflected the objectives and principles found elsewhere in PR studies more broadly – and in emancipatory projects in particular – that demonstrate clearly the importance of conferring control and ownership of data on to participants themselves, including the subsequent stages of research production. Such approaches provide the same opportunities to participants that academic researchers have in these processes. The benefits of this kind of emancipatory approach are that it can help to equalise or democratise research relationships and to effect transformations, whether these are personal, political, social, community-based, or all of these. The first of these benefits in PR – facilitating greater equality in researcher–participant relationships – has been demonstrated through close examination of the different kinds of participatory projects (for example, visual, visual-textual and narrative) described in the chapters of this book so far. However, this aspect of

PR also requires some further exploration, especially with respect to the opportunities PR offers for effective role transformations in research.

Equalising relationships and transforming researcher roles in participatory research

In PR, the experiences, perspectives and actions of participants (as storytellers, data producers, and so on) are prioritised over those of academic researchers to try and ensure that participants' narratives or stories or indeed, themselves as 'tellers' or authors, are not 'shut down' (Baldwin, 2013, p 105). Thus, in PR, researcher–participant relationships are not only equalised, but they are also reconfigured through a process of role transposition and transformation. In conventional research processes, the role and act of 'telling the story' in research is often what marks the distinction between the researcher and the 'researched', where the former's professionalised status is confirmed or underscored by the act of interpreting, constructing and re-presenting stories told in research (by participants) through the final written research story itself (in the form of, for example, end of project reports, books and journal publications written by academic researchers). Even in auto-ethnographic and reflexive approaches, where the intention is to redress power imbalances between researchers and research participants, it is hard to deny or overlook the dominance of the authorial 'voice' of the narrator, that is, the voice of the academic researcher-as-analyst/writer etc.

Indeed, Redwood (1999, p 674) makes a distinction between 'narrative' and 'story' in research processes: while she acknowledges the 'thrill from entering into another's story', and that stories thus become 'a form of social interaction', she also states that in terms of the different roles adopted in research and the narratives that are produced, 'the term "story" is usually used to describe what the actor tells and the "narrative" is the researchers' account'. Here, then, a distinction is made between who is doing the original storytelling (conventionally, the research participant) and who is responsible for, and takes ownership of, the data and the final research narrative (conventionally, the academic researcher) – a proposition that, as stated, is contested in more genuine participatory approaches to social research. While it is important not to underplay or deny completely the important role of the third-party academic researcher in the research process – in some cases, despite the best participatory or emancipatory intentions, their particular skills and expertise are essential in PR, and particularly in facilitating social change outcomes – what is important to understand is that practices that are commonly associated with the 'professional' researcher (research analysis, interpretation, writing and writing up) can *also* be assigned to, or assimilated effectively by, research participants themselves, as demonstrated in the PR studies discussed throughout this book.

In considering further the role of the academic researcher-as-writer in conventional qualitative studies, while numerous articles, books and so on discuss writing as a technique in research, more usually these discussions refer to the writing practices of 'professional'/academic researchers (and not of participants themselves) or to reflexive or auto-ethnographic approaches. It is common in these kinds of approaches, and in methodological discussions about them, for the act or phase of writing in research to be aligned with a certain kind of (academic or scientific) 'professionalism' or authoritative expertise, which, as stated, is usually assigned to the 'professional'/academic researcher-as-writer and not the research participant. Plummer's chapter in *Documents of life* (2001, chapter 8) on *writing life stories* is one such example, in which topics such as 'how to present a life story', 'the problem of writing', 'writing strategies' and so on relate to the role of the life story researcher and the challenges they might encounter. However, Plummer's review of critical humanist approaches in the form of life story research or 'documents of life' does lead him to conclude that different, more empathic and democratising approaches in research are needed:

> The problems of authors, voices and self then are complex. But they could lead us to consider the possibilities for creating relatively open and democratic texts when they contain a fluidity between subjects, researchers and selves. (Plummer, 2001, p 182)

A fundamental principle and intention in participatory and emancipatory research is to achieve the 'fluidity' to which Plummer refers, and to give the participants in research opportunities for being *actively* involved in research processes and practices, including data collection, analysis, writing and so on. It is equally important to allow research participants time to examine, consider and reflect on the data they produce. This worked well in the PNR study (as discussed above), and was equally successful in the photographic studies described in Chapters Two and Three. Indeed, I would propose that all research should involve participants in reflexive processes – to provide opportunities for assessing the methods used, the outputs from research, and so on (see also Hill, 2006).

Reflexivity in research

While from a participatory perspective such opportunities for reflection in research might be seen not only as important but imperative for those who take an *active* role in research participation – and certainly in terms of addressing power imbalances and attempting to democratise research–participant relationships – reflexivity is by no means a straightforward process. As Walmsley and Johnson (2003, p 39) propose, researchers often find this 'much more difficult to do in practice.' This may be because of uncertainties about the role reflexivity plays in research processes, or it may also be because reflexivity remains a somewhat contentious practice. Furthermore, where academic researchers themselves engage in reflexive practices in PR, without due consideration of the need to equalise and, in some cases, transform research relationships, there is always the risk that researchers' reflexive 'voices' may overshadow or challenge participant 'voice', thus fundamentally undermining the participatory principles and objectives of PR. Such outcomes can occur despite the claims made about reflexivity for democratising researcher–participant relationships and addressing power imbalances.

In auto-ethnographic research studies, as well as in other research contexts (and in different practice settings; see the discussion below), academic researchers themselves construct narratives of the self based on their own experiences of conducting research. These personalised accounts can provide ways of 'making sense of' or explicating research processes during fieldwork phases, for example (in the form of fieldwork notes or diaries; see Finlay, 2002), as well as useful observations about the nature of relationships between researchers, participants and the social world. Pillow (2003, p 181) refers to four reflexive research strategies in qualitative studies – 'reflexivity as recognition of self; reflexivity as recognition of other; reflexivity as truth; and reflexivity as transcendence' – which, she argues, are interdependent and as such offer the researcher confessional as well as cathartic opportunities, and provide 'a *cure for the problem of doing representation*' (Pillow, 2003, p 181; emphasis added). However, from a participatory perspective, such 'curative' opportunities are not necessarily (nor, in some cases, at all) realised simply by encouraging and enabling academic researchers to tell their own research stories or narratives.

While in one sense the contributions of the academic researcher as 'knower' and narrator are undoubtedly of value, and can contribute to our understanding of the social world and the ways in which knowledge is produced, looked at another way, the reflexive activities of academic researchers may also create ambiguity or uncertainty about authorship and whose story is being told or is of most value or significance. In participatory and emancipatory research methods, specifically, such ambiguity must be avoided; indeed, in PR, as stated, the intention is to transpose roles, or engage in a degree of role transference between participants and researchers depending on the level of participation involved or planned (see Chapter Six, Figure 6.1), and thus the aim is purposefully to deny, or at the very least mute, the 'voice' of the 'expert' academic researcher.

It is therefore important to note that despite calls by some for greater (academic) researcher reflexivity in social research studies, power dynamics in researcher–participant relationships are not necessarily overcome when academic researchers (as narrators) bring to the table their own lived experiences or knowledge of the social world. As Arnot and Reay (2007, p 318) argue, 'there are tense and often contradictory interactions between social voices and pedagogic voices, between dominant and dominated voice', and this can be equally true in respect of the voices of the (academic) researcher and 'the researched', even when the reflexive accounts of the former aim to contribute to our understanding of these power dynamics.

This is because these kinds of approaches – where academic researchers adopt reflexive authorial roles – may also serve to further 'professionalise' writing practices and, arguably, could help to create further polarity between the (expert) researcher and the ('non-expert') research participant. This is particularly true when academic researchers write reflexively about their own experiences in the field and these accounts then become part of the outputs from research, because without similar written representations from participants, the division between the (academic) researcher and the 'researched' (as well as the 'professionalised' status of the academic researcher) is further emphasised. Furthermore, one could also argue that the participatory and inclusive potential of social research studies are only undermined by an unequal approach to reflexive writing practice.

In feminist ethnography, reflexive practice has undoubtedly generated new and important dialogues about the methodological and epistemological challenges in social science research for the 'professional' researcher as well as for research participants. Nevertheless, concerns about the introspective and subjective nature of these kinds of reflexive observations remain. As Nagar and Geiger (2007, p 2) propose, these observations have tended to focus mainly 'on examining the identities of individual researchers rather than on how such identities intersect with institutional, geopolitical and material aspects of their positionality.' In her discussion about the contribution of ethnographic research in the social sciences, O'Reilly (2012, p 11) also recognises the importance of the accounts and reflexive observations of academic researchers themselves, but argues that research studies within the ethnographic tradition should also aim to promote understanding of 'social life as the outcome of the interaction of structure and agency through the practice of everyday life [and] with some analysis of wider structures, over time.'

However, some commentators reject completely the need for reflexivity among (academic) researchers, and claim that not only does reflexive engagement point to the self-indulgent, even vainglorious attempts of scholars to impress themselves into the 'story' of others, but that it can even serve to compromise the participatory or emancipatory objectives of research (see Patai, 1994; Pillow, 2003). Indeed, in her discussion of Patai's 'scathing critique' of reflexivity, Pillow (2003, p 176) underlines the tensions between what she describes as self-absorbed, 'privileged academics engaged in the erotics of their own language games' and how to faithfully represent the real problems and crises of people's lives. This distinction seems to be particularly apposite when considering participatory and emancipatory methods and principles in research, and the 'problem' of representation (in PR, this is overcome by providing opportunities for participants to reflect on and analyse their own data, as shown).

From the perspective of more inclusive approaches in PR, and particularly when working with vulnerable or marginalised participants, I would argue that, at the very least, reflexive exercises that are undertaken by researchers within the academy should contribute new methodological knowledge as well as new insights about researcher roles and relationships, and should not take precedence over participant perspectives. In PR specifically, the 'voices' of academic researchers should not subsume or be prioritised over those of research participants themselves; indeed, quite the opposite should be the case.

Taking my own research as an example, including the PNR study discussed in this and the previous chapter, as well as the research described and discussed in Chapters Two and Three, this represents to a large extent a journey through research processes and practice – through research design, methods, ethics, praxis, and so on – and hopefully contributes something new to knowledge and understanding about PR and working more effectively with vulnerable or marginalised people.

However, to some extent, what is also missing from my story or narrative as a researcher working within the academy, and specifically as a participatory researcher, are detailed descriptions of the time, energy and space needed to develop trusting relationships based on mutuality, understanding and empathy with research participants. One of the reasons for this is that this process is, in many respects, an intuitive one that cannot readily be taught or relayed in a formal, rule-driven way outside the field, so to speak. So while this process demands researchers who are appropriately skilled and experienced, it also requires a degree of instinctual knowledge, insight and empathy (or mutuality). These factors are essential to the success of the participatory project, and also critical in helping to foster and develop relationships of trust between researchers and participants, as well as understanding on the part of the academic researcher about their roles and place in these research relationships.

In order both to promote and achieve emancipatory objectives in PR, the processes described above often also necessitate (academic) researchers taking a step back in research relationships, in order to facilitate more genuinely inclusive and emancipatory approaches, as evidenced in the PNR study described in Chapter Four. Thus, embarking on this research journey, in many respects, requires the academic researcher to contribute new methodological, practical and other kinds of knowledge and insights that may be helpful to others. But it also demands recognition of the point at which authorial, analytical and reflexive expertise and precedence must be conceded to others who are the participants in research, and whose voices must be prioritised, especially if participants' lives and experiences – and data – are to be more faithfully presented rather than re-presented.

This kind of recognition and understanding about the nature and importance of research relationships in PR relies, then, on the expertise and particular skills of the experienced academic researcher, but also requires understanding and insight into the wishes and needs of participants, including their ability and willingness to take part in research studies that enhance participatory and even emancipatory principles and objectives. There is, of course, a considerable difference between people's ability and willingness to take part in research – including the numerous phases involved in research processes, from research design, data collection, analyses, writing up, and so on – and in many respects the former can be addressed and resolved by using different or less conventional methods that have been designed and discussed with participants themselves, in order to arrive at agreed methods that best suit their needs. The latter, on the other hand, becomes an issue of personal choice and, as has been argued throughout the preceding chapters, should be addressed through careful negotiation between (academic) researchers and participants, as well as through the application of appropriate ethical processes and ongoing dialogue and communication in more democratised researcher–participant relationships.

Transformative participation

The aim of PR, and PAR in particular, is, in the main, to be transformative with respect to social, political and cultural change that has a structural rather than a simply subjective element. However, where PR involves multiply vulnerable or marginalised individuals and groups it may not always be possible – or necessarily a specific research objective from the outset – to achieve these kinds of transformations. In some cases, the aim in PR may simply be to achieve personal transformations for participants themselves at a subjective or individualised level through, for example, the use of new and/or bespoke research methods themselves, as we have seen from some of the research projects described in previous chapters. In this sense, 'testing' certain research methodologies may be a fundamental aim of PR studies, that look to ascertain whether and how certain methods may bring about personal transformations – as was the case in the PNR study – and whether the success of these are reflected in practice settings, or are transferable in these contexts. In the PNR study, the therapeutic benefits of the participatory narrative (writing) method itself were clear, and indeed this was a key message to emerge from all the women who took part in the project. In Rosie's case, for example, the opportunity to write and publish her own story in full and to participate in the act of writing gave her a sense of closure on her experiences of domestic violence, as described above. One of the other women participants, Carla, also described (in writing) the PNR method and writing process as useful strategies for helping her name the abuse and to recognise it for what it was:

> Writing it down makes me realise it did happen and it does happen. And it shouldn't happen. I don't find it easy talking to anyone about this, writing about it felt easier in a way in that although I know someone would be reading it eventually, it still felt private in a way and they don't know who I am and I could write how I really felt and I was in control of writing it, no one else and that's important to me. And I know what I've written isn't going to be changed and it's mine; it's my story and it's real.

Notably, the importance of naming and recognising abuse among women victims of domestic violence, as well as using writing as a therapeutic device in practice as part of this naming process, are clear in the domestic violence literature and in broader literatures on trauma counselling, for example. Thus, outcomes from the PNR study with respect to the success of the method in helping women recognise, name and come to terms with the abuse reflect outcomes from domestic violence practice where similar methods are used (see, for example, Seeley and Plunkett, 2002). In terms of using these methods more broadly in other kinds of PR studies, there are also important synergies and opportunities in terms of the transferable nature of such methods – within and across different disciplines and in practice, for example.

More creative techniques for eliciting the experiences and perspectives of service users have also been used in therapeutic practice as a way of illuminating and addressing aspects of vulnerability, and as a way of gaining important insights into trauma and abuse issues, for example (see Bolton, 1999, 2010; Thompson, 2010). The use of personal stories or narrative methods have also been effective as pedagogic tools in health and social care practice, where professionals construct their own reflective narratives about their approaches to their work, and use these to inform and underpin inter- or intra-disciplinary practice. These types of approaches are commonly used in educational action research and in health or clinical settings (see, for example, Pennebaker, 2000; Bolton et al, 2006; Bolton, 2010). Bolton's (2006) work on reflective enquiry in educational practice, for example, engaged both professionals and students in poetry and story-writing as a critical learning experience. The intention was to use action-learning sets to examine teaching and learning experiences. Bolton concluded that this more personalised and creative process 'stimulated clarification of personal values and priorities, created a context for peer support (which doctors often seem to resist), and fostered recognition of opportunities to make constructive changes in their professional lives ...' (2006, p 216).

Pritchard and Sainsbury (2004) describe ways of using creative writing techniques in practice with child and adult victims of abuse through the use of journal writing and compilation, and poetry (for similar approaches in sports-based research, see Sparkes and Douglas, 2007; see also Poindexter, 2002). In many respects, the process of story-writing/narrative construction in these settings, as well as the more immediate and direct involvement of service users in 'telling' their stories, are considered more important or of greater value than the end product itself, at least in the initial stages. Participants (whether these are service users, patients or professionals) are encouraged to write first and foremost for themselves, and not for an imagined readership or audience (see Bolton et al, 2011). Pritchard and Sainsbury's work with abused and traumatised children and adults thus fosters a process of objectifying traumatic experiences but also enables participants to 'regain control over their feelings and, thus, their lives' (2004, p 11).

These different ways of eliciting individualised narratives or stories (or narratives of the self; see Chapter One), through creative writing and storytelling practices in health, social care, education and in social work (see Fraser, 2004; Baldwin, 2013), can have personal health and therapeutic benefits for those who take part. Furthermore, such outcomes can also translate into social and political transformations, both for individuals and groups or communities. Haaken, for example, uses feminist psychoanalytical perspectives and storytelling techniques to uncover women's experiences and accounts of domestic violence and other forms of abuse as a way of making both personal and political transformations. In her book, *Hard knocks: Domestic violence and the psychology of storytelling* (Haaken, 2010), evidence was gathered from more than 200 interviews with women victims–survivors of domestic violence, with the outcome that 'storytelling served as the portal of entry to [background] knowledge – that might be termed the *social unconscious* of the movement – and to forms of collective remembering that may be useful in thinking through present dilemmas' (Haaken, 2010, p 3). Thus, although Haaken does not make participatory claims about her research, the women's *individual* stories, as well as her analyses of films, novels, self-help books and so on, are used *collectively* and in a transformative way to consider contemporary debates and dilemmas in domestic violence epistemologies and practice (see also Allen, 2011).

Taking the domestic violence movement as a case study, Lehrner and Allen (2008, p 220) note 'the central role of meaning-making' in facilitating social change, and the way in which understanding of domestic violence has shifted from an individual issue or problem to a broader social, and political concern, which is intrinsically linked to patriarchy and issues of inequality. On the face of it, this would appear to contradict or create a point of tension in terms of the kinds of qualitative research methods that have emphasised individualised, even subjective, approaches, such as those used in the PNR study, for example. However, there is also recognition in broader analyses of social movements that there is a commitment to shared narratives, or what Fine describes as 'a bundle of narratives' (1995, p 128, cited in Lehrner and Allen, 2008). Thus, we can see that, in terms of social change objectives in research and in social movements and social activism, there is some synergy between research that seeks to facilitate 'voice' at an individual level, but which also attempts to 'collectivise' evidence in order to facilitate social change, and social movements more broadly that seek to do the same. As Lehrner and Allen conclude, 'researchers have emphasized the role of individuals in shaping the ideology of their setting and of the larger movement' (2008, p 222).

The parallels are clear, then, between individualised approaches to eliciting information based on personal experience that are used in practice or in social movements – for facilitating voice and influencing personal transformations – and PR methods and approaches that aim to do the same. These parallels represent, in effect, the 'virtuous circle' of research and practice, that is, they show how the qualities and potential of PR and different inclusive and individualised (bottom-up) methods can have considerable relevance and value in practice settings, and vice versa. Thus, individualised participant-, patient- or service user-led approaches such as storytelling, life history or autobiographical and creative writing and visual methods not only facilitate a process of 'coming to know' the 'self', but also a process of understanding, and influencing the 'system'. They also allow individual voices to be heard and understood in broader social, political and cultural contexts. Similar processes and outcomes are also mirrored in practice. For example, in Seeley and Plunkett's (2002) *Standards for counselling practice* in domestic violence work, the authors used information provided by individual women victims of domestic violence about their counselling experiences, undertook a comprehensive literature review, and set up a consultation process in order to formulate the practice standards. The authors also state, 'this process was informed by the reports of victim's/survivor's experience of counselling, research data and current theoretical perspectives and the field experiences of the researchers' (2002, p 2).

Transformative potential of participatory research: some issues and challenges

It is important, however, not to get too carried away with the idea that less conventional participatory methods may lead to social, political or cultural transformations for individuals at this broader level. In many cases, researchers may have to content themselves with transformations on a much smaller, subjective scale, and there are a number of reasons for this. At an individual level, for example, despite the best participatory intentions of academic researchers, some participants may be unable or unwilling to engage with more creative methods that put them at the heart of the 'storytelling' process, or to recall and relate their experiences in narrative ways (either in written, visual or visual-textual form, for example). Thus, in PR, methodological decisions will need to consider and take account of participants' cognitive abilities, as well as their literacy and motor skills, and also whether they have been given the necessary educational opportunities in order to describe, write about or translate their experiences in the ways that the methods demand. As discussed in Chapter Three, consideration of participants' cognitive abilities are important in terms of ascertaining whether, and to what extent, they are able to translate ideas or thoughts, based on knowledge about their personal experiences and the social world, into the spoken, written or visual form. Where research and (academic) researchers do not take account of such considerations and issues, the transformative potential – both personally for participants themselves and politically, culturally, and so on – will be considerably reduced.

Alongside such practical considerations, it is also necessary to address more abstract and philosophical ideas and arguments. Some commentators have argued, for example, that there is a natural distinction in both human nature and character that means some people are 'natural' narrators and others not. Despite arguments from social anthropologists, sociologists and psychologists that people are inherently storytellers and that telling personal stories (in whatever form) is a natural *social* process (see Ellis and Bochner, 1992; Lieblich et al, 1998), others claim that some people simply do not translate personal experience and consciousness into stories or in narrative ways. Strawson (2004), for example, argues that the view that human consciousness or 'self' is invented or created through storytelling or narrative expression is only partially true for some people and entirely false for others. In fact, Strawson claims that 'there is a deep divide in our species' between narrators and non-narrators. The first are 'intensely narrative, storytelling, Homeric, in their sense of life and self', and the second are 'those who live life in a fundamentally non-storytelling fashion, who may have little sense of, or interest in, their own history' (p 15).

However, Strawson's view that narrative constructions of human experience can also be psychologically damaging, and the idea that somehow human subjects would be better off without self-reflection or memorial focus, fails to offer an alternative way of living or eliciting human consciousness and experience, and also seems to suggest a rather pessimistic outlook for the human condition. Furthermore, this perspective overlooks entirely the evidence that storytelling (including writing and reflexive practices, as well as other visually-based approaches in research and in practice) can be personally transforming and beneficial therapeutically for many people, including those who may not have thought of themselves either as 'natural' narrators or storytellers. This is certainly clear from evidence from health, social care and education practice as well as from research studies such as those described in this and previous chapters of this book (whether this be in the form of oral, visual or written narratives), and in particular those that adopt an emancipatory approach. Indeed, one of the fundamental ways of addressing some of the challenges in PR is to work *with* participants, to engage with them in ongoing dialogue and consultation in order to identify ways of facilitating memorial and narrative performance using the most appropriate methods.

In terms of broader, structural contexts, there is also the issue of the perceived value and 'credibility' of data that are, for example, produced and analysed by participants themselves. There is undoubtedly some tension between these kinds of data and those that are collated, analysed and presented by the 'professional' academic researcher. This is particularly apparent in certain applied fields (in social policy research, for example; see Walker et al, 2008) where statistical (quantitative) evidence that is collated, analysed and interpreted by academic researchers is often accorded greater 'scientific' status than (qualitative) data based on individualised accounts provided and presented by participants themselves. This may be even more apparent when such data are collated and presented by vulnerable or marginalised participants – for example, people whose stories may not be 'welcomed' or believed, or are 'shut down', as Baldwin describes (2013, p 105).

It is also more likely that the value and even the accuracy or 'truth' of research accounts and data that have been collated and presented by research participants themselves are more likely to be questioned or be subject to closer scrutiny than the reflections and research narratives (including 'data' and 'findings' narratives) of 'professional' researchers. It can, of course, be argued that the credibility of research methods and research projects themselves are 'tested' in other ways, for example, considerations of methodological rigour through peer review processes.

Of course, there are valid reasons for demanding research be subject to independent assessment and analysis by third-party professional researchers, which are inevitably influenced by assumptions and expectations about objectivity. The value of PR, however, lies in the opportunities it presents to involve participants in different ways that enhance collaboration – including during data analysis and reflexive stages – as well as the potential for conferring ownership over research data and processes within, for example, larger, multi-method studies.

Furthermore, the advantages of PR and its associated methods also lie in its capacity to challenge conventional research approaches that over time become a matter of custom or common practice. Such set ways of thinking can mean that the authenticity, value and credibility of participant stories or narratives (in whatever form), particularly those collated using less conventional methods and conducted among small numbers of individual participants, may be called into question, or may not be considered sufficiently or appropriately 'scientific'. As Crosby and colleagues (2010, p 3) suggest:

> It is important to consider whether there is a tendency within our discipline to overvalue findings derived from large samples and undervalue findings stemming from small samples. Such bias could inadvertently steer research away from studies involving under-served and hard to reach populations.

While there is clearly a danger in making presumptions about authenticity in research that works more inclusively and directly with participants themselves – as Ezzy (1998, p 169) has argued, qualitative methodologies more generally 'often assume reported data accurately reflects the realities of lived experience' – at the very least, participatory approaches that promote participant 'voice', and that allow for subjective experiential data and interpretations both to underpin and inform our understanding about social words and knowledge production, can and do make important contributions here. They can certainly help steer research more generally towards, rather than away from, studies and methods that enhance participation among multiply vulnerable or 'hard-to-reach' populations (see Crosby et al, 2010, p 3).

Thus, while research evidence that has been produced by participants themselves (including multiply vulnerable individuals and groups) may not always be considered credible or of equal value to the kinds of evidence produced by the 'professional' academic researcher (and particularly in certain applied contexts), there are other ways of addressing and enhancing the transformative potential of PR. One way of doing this would be to consider more long-term objectives – transformative outcomes need not always be immediately tangible or non-contingent, and may involve academic researchers taking an active role in trying to effect change. For example, research on developing or emerging subjects, and particularly when it is conducted among vulnerable or marginalised populations, can take time to evolve and transform thinking, policy and practice, as well as people's lives.

To give an example here, Ezzy's (1998) narrative study of the experiences of vulnerable people living with HIV/AIDS focused on the personal account of just one man, Scott, who was living with HIV/AIDS at that time. Meaning-making, identity and selfhood were explored through Scott's written narrative which allowed for a 'reconsideration of how [Scott] sees his past as a consequence of a changed understanding of the future' (1998, p 174). While the study focused on just a single case study, Ezzy was able to use the data to contribute new knowledge in terms of developing public health discourses, and other evidence, on HIV/AIDS *over time* as a result of further consideration of existing and developing evidence and knowledge about the impact of HIV/AIDS.

With respect to these and other kinds of transformations in PR, there are a number of other ways of addressing and overcoming the inherent challenges and dilemmas that arise when attempting to conduct PR with vulnerable or marginalised groups in order to effect change (see also Aldridge, 2013). These include:

- Enhancing the role of researchers (whether these are academic or participant-researchers) as advocates in PR where necessary, and appropriate, and specifically in helping to communicate the messages from research (see also the discussion in Chapter Three).
- Introducing participatory methods with vulnerable, marginalised participants in multi-method studies to facilitate different analytical and reflexive processes, as well as different strategies and approaches to communicating the messages from research.
- Looking for patterns across datasets in PR studies to contribute new knowledge and effect transformations over time.
- Promoting the wider use of PR that is clearly and rigorously designed and implemented using appropriate and recognised participatory models (see Chapter Six).

The above principles and actions are not only relevant in the context of the PR studies described and discussed throughout the chapters of this book, but also to PR more generally. However, the issue of clearly designed and rigorous participatory methods with respect to formal PR models is something that I address specifically in the sixth and final chapter of the book.

Conclusion

Booth has argued that, despite the best of intentions, (academic) researchers are often drawn into 'betraying their subjects by representing them' (1996, p 243), through the process of (third-party) interpretation or 'amanuensis'. While analysis and interpretation are both recognised and necessary processes in any or all kinds of research, whether in qualitative or quantitative studies, there is, undoubtedly, a role for participants to play in helping to address the tensions that present themselves here. This is certainly the case when participants are given sole or co-analytical roles in research and when they are given opportunities to reflect on the data they have produced. Furthermore, from a participatory perspective, there is undeniably a loss of immediacy, evocation and, perhaps more importantly, faithfulness, with respect to the analysis and interpretation of personal stories or narratives in research through the intercession of a (third-party) academic researcher.

In many respects, PR methods and approaches rely on and demand a degree of flexibility in research processes, including a less structured or formulaic approach to analysis and interpretation (see, for example, Fraser, 2004; Poindexter, 2002). Furthermore, with respect to standard or conventional tests of research in terms of their reliability and validity, Booth (1996, p 253) argues that these 'are neither appropriate nor adequate when lives are not consistent, biographical truth is a "will-o'-the-wisp" and stories inevitably reflect something of the teller.' Thus, as has been shown, PR has an important role to play in facilitating individual voices and stories, especially when such voices are more likely either to be overlooked or silenced in conventional research studies.

With respect to the transformative potential of PR, there may appear to be somewhat of a contradiction between methods and approaches that allow for a degree of subjectivity as well as analytical freedom, and the call for greater rigour with respect to PR design and principles. However, it is important for researchers to understand the distinctions here, particularly when working with and including vulnerable or marginalised participants in research. As stated, such participant groups need to be included in research in ways that are appropriate and effective for them which requires researchers to take a 'bottom-up' (even bespoke) participatory approach to research design and implementation. However, this does not mean that researchers (whether academic researchers or participant-researchers) should surrender research objectives and principles that are aligned to recognised models of working just because the methods used are not conventional or customary within the qualitative field. This is an important issue to which I turn in the following concluding chapter.

SIX

Advancing participatory research

Issues and challenges in participatory research

This chapter draws together some of the key issues to emerge from the previous chapters regarding the advantages and challenges in PR in order to advance participatory methods and approaches. With this advancement in mind, this chapter also considers the need to posit or locate participatory methods more broadly (including PAR, PNR, and so on, with vulnerable or marginalised groups) within a defined Participatory Model (PM). Such a model is constructed and presented (see Figure 6.1) from a participant-oriented standpoint, and is intended as an aid to researchers (and others) who are planning, or reflecting on the use of, participatory methods with different participant populations, including vulnerable, marginalised or socially excluded people. The PM and associated principles presented and described below are also intended to highlight and promote issues of 'voice' and emancipation in qualitative research more broadly. While as Walmsley and Johnson suggest, qualitative research techniques such as case studies, interviews and stories appear to offer opportunities for 'increasing power for participants', they also note that 'not all qualitative research is concerned with empowering those who take part in it' (2003, p 32).

What is missing from research that facilitates participatory approaches are guidelines, or a frame of reference, from which researchers (and practitioners) can work in order to enhance collaboration, inclusion and emancipation in research relationships, and particularly with vulnerable or marginalised groups, as well in the processes and practice of PR itself. While the focus of this book has not been specifically on PAR, which tends to focus on large or small *group* dynamics (see Chevalier and Buckles, 2013, p 10; see also Chapter One) and *community* action and transformation, rather than marginalised or socially excluded individuals, nevertheless, some of the underlying principles of PAR are shared with PR more broadly. This is particularly the case in participatory approaches that consider and work with participants as actors in research (see Figure 6.1) – and especially in terms of 'doing research "with people", in lieu of doing it "on them"' (Chevalier and Buckles, 2013, p 10).

Any proposed participatory framework or model will require commitment from researchers to recognise and adhere to a number of *principles* and objectives when conducting the kinds of research that make participatory claims, rather than working within a strict set of *rules*. As discussed in Chapter Five, during analytical and interpretive phases in PR, strict formulas or techniques should be surrendered in favour of more flexible, and indeed, generous, ways of working with or 'reading' data (including narrative, visual or orally produced data). As discussed, principles of participation in PR should also ensure greater equity in researcher–participant relationships (including and particularly when participants are vulnerable, marginalised or socially excluded), and engagement in dialogue with participants as part of an ongoing process throughout the duration of research studies.

Qualitative research methods generally facilitate closer working relationships with human subjects, with the intention of collating data that reflects this important human dimension in research. We have already seen how diverse PR studies and methodologies within this qualitative tradition have generated different types of research data, including narratives in the form of personal stories, in visual form, as visual-textual data, as well as in the form of written narratives. These kinds of methods and approaches that are constructed and articulated as spoken, written or visualised narratives produced by participants themselves in autobiographical form can then serve as 'a starting point for developing further understandings of the social construction of each person's subjectivity' (Goodson, 2013, p 30). While it is acknowledged that vulnerable or marginalised groups specifically are often not readily able to access or work with (self-produced) autobiographical methods that result in, for example, published written works, it is also recognised that as a research method, autobiographical techniques (and these can and should also include oral and visual methods) 'probably [hold] the greatest potential for full and equal partnership' (Walmsley and Johnson, 2003, p 149). This is because such methods and approaches emphasise and promote the participant-as-narrator as the expert or 'ultimate insider' (Walmsley and Johnson, 2003, p 149; see also Dwyer, 1982; Burgos-Debray, 1984; Kaplan, 1997; Etherington, 2000; Plummer, 2001).

In planning PR projects, whichever method is chosen or deemed to be most suitable, the process of data collection will in every case demand a level of recall and memory performance on the part of participants (see Aldridge and Dearden, 2013), as well as the capacity, and willingness, to translate these recollections into the spoken or written word, or in visual form, as (data) narratives. Thus, the transformative potential of research will depend to a large extent on the appropriateness and efficacy of the research design and methods used.

For some participants, talking about their experiences, in interviews or focus groups, for example, so that these accounts can be recorded and later transcribed, analysed and interpreted as data, will be appropriate and even welcomed. For others, different kinds of data collection methods will be necessary, particularly for those individuals who are more likely to be left out of research altogether, perhaps because they are deemed too difficult to identify and recruit on to studies that use conventional qualitative methods, or because their particular vulnerabilities or needs mean such methods are not appropriate.

As demonstrated in the in-depth discussion of the various PR projects described in some detail in Chapters Two through to Five of this book, the kinds of participatory methods that will be more appropriate for people who are vulnerable or marginalised in some way (or ways) should allow for a considerable degree of flexibility and creativity in terms of research design and implementation. As well as giving participants opportunities for having a say in the kinds of methods used, PR should also provide them with opportunities for analysing (or co-analysing) and reflecting on the data they produce, the methods used and the participatory experience itself. In some cases, the kinds of methods introduced will provide participants with opportunities for engagement at most if not all of the stages of research production. They may also allow for both participants *and* their data to 'speak for themselves', to some extent, while at the same time offering unique and highly personalised insights into subjective experience.

Sometimes, such insights will raise more questions than answers. For example, where visual data are presented 'as is', so to speak (see Chapters Two and Three), or where narratives are produced in full, as was the case in the PNR study discussed in Chapters Four and Five, one question might be, do these kinds of approaches, that treat the participant as actor, as 'doer' (see Figure 6.1), tell us something different or unique about the actor (the participant-as-researcher) and their experiences? In the PNR study these kinds of questions were especially pertinent, not least because we know so little about the experiences and needs of unsupported women victims of domestic violence. The women's self-authored accounts give us, then, direct entry into those experiences as well as contribute new knowledge in relatively uncharted territory.

The aim of participatory or emancipatory projects such as these is to confer control over the 'telling' and ownership of the data on to participants, and to give them opportunities to present something of *themselves* as participants, narrators and researchers (and thus to avoid the risk of misinterpretation or misrepresentation). Opportunities for self-enhancement are augmented when participants are more directly involved in research that facilitates autobiographical (self)-elicitation, in whatever form. While it is also important to allow participants (as researchers) to engage in analytical and reflexive processes, it is also the case that readers and viewers will, to a large extent, undertake their own interpretations of texts, visual images, and so on, especially where these are presented simply 'as is', in which case, it is not always sufficient for participant-researchers to present their data in these ways, although this depends, of course, on the context in which they are produced and made available.

The reason for presenting Rosie's narrative from the PNR study in Chapter Four, in full and unedited form, was first to allow the reader to form her or his own interpretation of the narrative. Examples of the kinds of narrative analyses that *could* be conducted by a third party were then presented in Chapter Five, but also, and importantly, alongside examples from Rosie's *own* reflections and analysis. This multi-stage approach allows the reader to compare their own considerations of the narrative with these different interpretations. Such an approach mirrors that of Lieblich and colleagues (1998) who, in their book, *Narrative research: Reading, analysis, and interpretation*, present two complete participant narratives so that readers can interpret and analyse the texts themselves, as well as compare the authors' interpretations against the actual text. In many respects, in a book of this kind, on which the focus is PR methods, such flexibility (and, to some extent, experimentation) with respect to the ways in which research evidence is presented, considered, analysed, and so on, can be readily accommodated, especially when the intention is to demonstrate how researchers can 'push forward the boundaries of what is possible' (Lewis and Porter, 2004, p 192).

Developing a Participatory Model

In considering all of the above issues with respect to PR and working more effectively with vulnerable or marginalised people, we can see the value in shifting to a more personal, individualised approach in order to gain deeper insight into human consciousness, experience and need. The methods used to elicit this kind of information such as autobiography, story-'telling', life histories using oral, written or visual techniques, and other creative methods (see, for example, Gray and Sinding, 2002; Sparkes and Douglas, 2007), as well as reflexive techniques and so on, are best suited to this sort of subjective, individualised approach and to facilitating closer and more collaborative relationships between academic researchers and participants (as well as in practice, between professionals and service users or patients, for example).

However, with regard to PR specifically, it is clear that not all research that adopts these kinds of methods or techniques lays claim to or aligns itself with a strict or clearly defined participatory approach. On the other hand, as has been stated already, some PR studies make participatory claims without explicating the nature, extent or limitations of participation involved, and particularly from the perspective of participants themselves. This is clearly unhelpful in terms of promoting and advancing PR as a way of working more effectively with participants, including vulnerable or marginalised individuals or groups. Indeed, researchers, and other interested parties, should not have to search for participatory indicators in descriptions of research studies that claim to use and promote inclusive or emancipatory ways of working. The kinds of participatory methods used, as well as the design and context of the research and the relevant theoretical underpinnings, should be clear from the outset in PR projects, as should the ways in which participatory and, where relevant, emancipatory, principles and objectives will be achieved through working collaboratively and inclusively with participants.

There are a number of reasons why such clarity is required, not least of which is to avoid research that is tokenistic or simply pays lip service to participatory or emancipatory principles and aims. As Lewis and Porter (2004, p 196) argue, if we are committed to 'giving voice' in research, then the process demands 'careful planning, preparation and the apportioning of appropriate time', as well as the need to 'keep asking ourselves *what trust we can place in our methods* and check we have not overly predetermined the views that we have encouraged to be heard' (emphasis added).

A further reason is that (academic) researchers must demonstrate commitment, not only to the participants in research (as well as to the academy and to research funders; see Aldridge, 2012b), but also to developing and advancing PR methods in order to enhance the credibility and rigour of these kinds of qualitative approaches. We know that studies that use less conventional and more creative methods in qualitative research are not so readily embraced in all contexts – in social policy, for example (see Walker et al, 2008). There is therefore even greater need for PR to achieve the kind of rigour and cohesion that has been called for in other related disciplines and fields. In the late 1990s, Lieblich and colleagues proposed that narrative research and methods, for example, required 'a deliberate investment of effort in the elucidation of working rules for such studies' (1998, p 1). These same requirements are also relevant today with respect to PAR, for example (as discussed in Chapter One; see also Chevalier and Buckles, 2013) and, I would argue, in terms of PR more generally, but with the emphasis on participatory *principles* and *models* of working rather than on strict 'rules' or formulas.

A further reason why there is a need for a more cohesive approach to PR based on sound principles and frameworks is that without this there is a danger that unrealistic or even half-hearted attempts will be made to work more collaboratively and inclusively with certain participant groups (including vulnerable or marginalised participants), thus further undermining the credibility of PR methods. This is not to suggest that important advances have not already been made in PR and in working more empathically and inclusively with participants who have traditionally been left out of research studies altogether; having said this, there is perhaps even greater need for care and attention to these matters (that is, to the principles and methods in PR processes) during times of such serious fiscal retrenchment that may mean research studies that are not considered sufficiently 'scientific' or 'credible' may be at even greater risk of being overlooked in a competitive and increasingly restrictive funding environment.

In such contexts it is even more pressing to try to ensure that vulnerable or marginalised people are included in 'mainstream' studies that can also accommodate or allow for a degree of methodological flexibility. Incorporating qualitative methods and, more specifically, clearly defined and designed PR techniques as part of a multi-method approach is one way of achieving this. This would ensure that those who have been left out of, or have had very little input into, research or public policy decision-making processes, could be included in ways that, as Hill and colleagues (2004, p 78) argue, 'meet their wishes and felt needs' through 'multi-dimensional participation'. This would help to ensure that vulnerable or marginalised people are included in both research and decision-making processes.

In further considering the ways in which greater clarity and methodological rigour can be brought to PR, what is missing from many studies that make participatory claims, as discussed, is recognition of the nature, extent and limitations of participation within individual projects. While various participatory typologies and models of working have been described and proposed in PAR specifically (see Biggs, 1989; Hart, 1992, 2008; Chevalier and Buckles, 2013), there have been few attempts to evaluate their efficacy, use and relevance in the field, particularly by participants themselves, or to bring these together under a broader PR banner. Neither do many studies that make participatory claims align themselves with specific participatory models or frames of reference.

The PM presented and discussed in this chapter (see Figure 6.1) has been developed with the intention of addressing some, if not all, of these issues and oversights by providing a participatory framework for researchers (and professionals/practitioners) to locate their own participatory projects with reference to the various domains within (and across) the model. Drawing extensively on my own experiences of conducting PR or participatory-type projects, as well as evidence from a wide range of other research studies in this field, the PM has been designed for the purpose of helping researchers more clearly align or define their PR projects with reference to, or across, a particular domain or domains within the model itself. The PM (presented from the perspective of participants) allows for a degree of transference between domains, thus some participatory projects may contain elements that traverse or intersect with the different domains.

However, the underlying principle is that research should always move *away from* tokenistic methods that treat participants as (passive) objects (the 'participant as object', PAO, domain in the model; see Figure 6.1), and especially in any kind of research that adopts or lays claim to PR methods and approaches. Thus, the PAO (tokenistic) domain is included in order to serve as a point *from* which PR should always advance. At the same time it is recognised that it is not always possible for research to be solely or strictly inclusive or 'emancipatory' ('participant-led', PL) – some research is designed without consultation with participants, but may then involve further elements of participatory design, either through greater collaboration with participants during fieldwork phases or during the outputs phase, for example. Thus, some research may contain participatory elements, where participants are treated as individual subjects ('participant as subject', PAS; see Figure 6.1), as well as other participatory elements (across the domains) that facilitate closer collaboration in research processes and relationships (for example, the 'participant as actor', PAA, domain). The PL domain prioritises social change outcomes as well as methods and approaches that facilitate and promote participant voice, self-advocacy and emancipation, and that also ensures participants themselves design and lead research projects wherever possible.

The PM has been designed to provide researchers (and practitioners) with a frame of reference from which they can develop their ideas and

Participatory research

Figure 6.1: Participatory Model

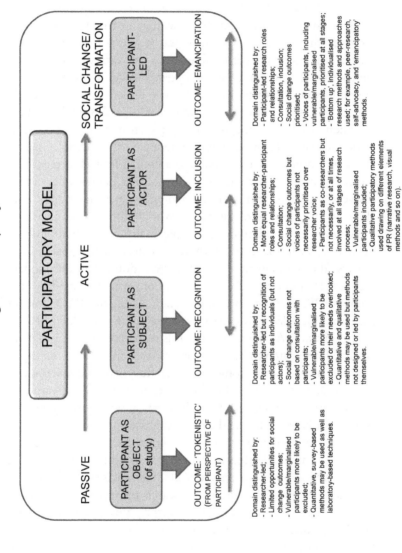

156

plans for working more inclusively with different population groups. As well as providing a measure or guide for future projects, the PM can also be used to evaluate past and current studies. Taking the participatory projects described and discussed in previous chapters as examples here, we can see that the early qualitative projects on young carers (see Chapter Two) would be located within the PAS domain, with some potential crossover into the PAA domain. The young carer/ mental health photographic research fits more clearly in the PAA field, but also with some elements borrowed from the PL domain. The PNR study described in Chapter Four is more obviously located with the PL field, although again, some elements are also evident within PAA – as stated, the purpose of the PM is to allow for such crossovers, or fluidity, within and across the model.

Principles of participation

An important aspect of the PM is that it provides researchers with a point of reference and an opportunity to more carefully consider the type of participatory methods and approaches that are possible, and to give greater consideration to the participatory claims that are made in research. Such claims should be verified or validated through careful explanation about the extent and limitations of the specific participatory approach adopted in research. Reference to participatory frameworks, typologies or models, such as the PM described in Figure 6.1, would undoubtedly help in this respect. For those researchers who are thinking about or planning PR, and particularly with vulnerable or marginalised participants, moving away from research that is tokenistic and which treats participants simply as objects and even as subjects in research (the PAO and PAS domains in the PM) would help advance PR methods and approaches that facilitate participant inclusion, collaboration and emancipation. Thus, alongside the PM, the following principles are proposed as a further guide or reference point for researchers (and professionals/practitioners) when thinking about and planning participatory projects (and particularly at the PAA and PL stages; see Figure 6.1). In these contexts, PR should:

- Be designed with the needs of participants in mind – it should take account of the needs of participants, their conditions and circumstances (including the nature and extent of their vulnerability or marginalisation, as well as social exclusion factors, where relevant).
- Involve a process of ongoing dialogue and consultation; this should include discussion of research design issues, the needs and

rights of participants, and how 'voice' is facilitated and can lead to transformative outcomes, as well as ethical issues and requirements.

- Ensure research relationships are based on mutuality, understanding and trust and, depending on the nature and extent of the participatory principles and objectives (what is achievable and realistic in research terms), that the voices of participants are prioritised over those of academic researchers.

- Be clear about the opportunities for participation, as well as the extent and limitations of the participatory approach, so that research projects do not raise unrealistic expectations for participants or make false participatory claims. It is essential that PR projects are clearly defined with respect to participatory typologies or participatory models/frameworks.

- Ensure participants are given opportunities to reflect on their engagement in research projects, as well as the level/extent or limitations of the participatory methods and approach. In this way, the views of participants must 'inform the link between social inclusion and participation' (Hill et al, 2004, p 80). Academic researchers may also want to be reflexive about research processes and relationships in order to make useful contributions to methods debates and discourses.

- Be sufficiently flexible so that participatory techniques may be included in larger, mainstream, multi-dimensional studies. PR methods can be effective in studies that adopt multi-method approaches, and this is especially the case when less conventional PR strategies are used, and when working with vulnerable or marginalised people.

- Recognise that vulnerability (marginalisation or social exclusion) is both a mutable and contestable concept, and that for most people, vulnerability is not a fixed identity or condition. PR should address vulnerability in this way and attempt to redress the impact of vulnerability or social exclusion, for example, through transformative objectives.

- Recognise that transformative outcomes can be personal, social, political, and so on, and may occur immediately, indirectly and/ or over time.

- Recognise that data that are collated and/or produced by participants in PR can be subject to different kinds of analyses, interpretation and reflexive processes; these should serve to enhance participant 'voice' and ensure that participants are not just treated as the objects of research, but are also considered as co-researchers, collaborators, disseminators, 'doers' and self-advocates within what is realistically achievable in PR terms.

Conclusion

As Barton and Papen (2002, p 69) have argued, the development of new and innovative methodologies in social research offers 'ways of working and writing in societies ... that contain possibilities [for] authenticity.' Haaken also proposes that narrative or storytelling techniques specifically (from a psychoanalytical perspective) provide opportunities for 'individual and social transformation' (2010, p 2). These different and more creative methods and approaches in PR, and the possibilities they offer, have been demonstrated throughout this book. One of the primary objectives of using narrative research methods, for example, in respect of framing and facilitating qualitative methods in social research, is to understand the relationship between experiential (subjective) evidence and its elicitation or expression in narrative form. Furthermore, the ways in which narratives are 'told' or elicited vary considerably, and can include, for example, visual or visual-textual narratives and creative arts-based approaches, as described in the various research projects discussed in the preceding chapters of this book.

As has also been shown, the advantages of these kinds of individualised approaches have also been noted in practice. For example, Fraser (2004) describes the democratising aspects of personal stories and autobiographical accounts told by 'ordinary' people, as well as their capacity to subdue what she refers to as the 'posturing inclinations of experts'. She adds, 'with the capacity to recognise people's strengths and engage people in active, meaning-making dialogues, narrative approaches ... may help social workers move beyond a strict problem focus to more generally explore social phenomena' (2004, p 181).

In qualitative research more broadly, methods have become increasingly creative to such a degree that it is not always possible to identify research that doesn't promote, embrace or include some form of narrative or story. However, the association between narrative research and life history or life story/autobiographical methods is particularly notable (discussed in detail in Chapter Four). Furthermore, the emphasis on the personal, small-scale narrative or story is also congruent and fits neatly with the broader principles and objectives of PR (and in practice), particularly with vulnerable or marginalised groups, which often necessitate and indeed embrace an in-depth approach with relatively small numbers of participants.

However, this does not mean that methods of working in PR using recognised models or frames of reference should be foresworn; far from it. Such frameworks, and principles in PR, should, indeed, be strengthened so that participatory methodologies and techniques can sit happily and credibly alongside those in other fields and disciplines that have established models of working and best practice. At the heart of all PR, and a core principle in both enhancing and advancing participatory and emancipatory methods, should be the perspectives of participants themselves, and 'the single human voice, telling its own story' (Lodge, 2002).

Notes

Chapter One

[1] It is less common in qualitative studies generally, however, including in ethnographic studies and even in participatory action and narrative investigations, for stories or accounts to be *written* by research participants themselves as the authors of their own accounts *and reproduced in their original form* (see Chapter Four).

[2] With respect to the use of personal or individual research stories or narratives, this is illustrated and perhaps even further complicated by Ezzy's proposition that a more sophisticated approach to (individualised) narrative or storytelling techniques 'does not treat narrative interpretations as disengaged from an obdurate reality, but neither should the question of the veracity of a narrative be dealt with by attempting to find objective indicators, uninfluenced by subjective interpretations' (1998, p 170; see also the further discussion in Chapters Four and Five).

[3] So, for example, where researchers work with research participants, as co-researchers, where research projects are designed jointly and participants are involved at each stage of the research process (see Walmsley and Johnson, 2003).

Chapter Two

[1] Franklin (2002) argues, for example, that the emphasis on children's criminality gained prominence and momentum in the early 1990s (with coverage of the urban riots and 'joy riding'), culminating in the 'child killers' rhetoric sparked by the murder of James Bulger in 1993 by two teenage boys, Jon Venables and Robert Thompson.

[2] Interestingly, Hill himself has conducted research into children's views about their participation in research, something he observes is a much less common practice even in research studies that adopt participatory methods and approaches (see the discussion in Chapters Five and Six).

[3] Indeed, in the recently published *Ethical research involving children* (ERIC) compendium (Graham et al, 2013), the key focus is on 'harm and benefits', 'informed consent', 'privacy and confidentiality' and 'compensation and

payments'. Throughout the compendium itself the views and perspectives of children and young people themselves are noticeably absent.

[4] It has also meant that research with children and young people has, until more recently, tended to treat children as objects or subjects in research rather than as participants or co-researchers (see Christensen and Prout, 2002).

[5] Clark herself, for example, acknowledges some of the challenges and complexities involved in undertaking research of this kind. Nevertheless, the methods she and her colleagues have developed have been extremely valuable in helping very young children participate in research.

[6] It can be argued that both methodological and theoretical alignments need to be made more clear in research that makes participatory claims; otherwise, the critical participatory elements in research will be obfuscated, generalised or will simply be tokenistic or false.

[7] 'Young carers are children and young people under the age of 18 who provide care, assistance or support to another family member. Young carers carry out, often on a regular basis, significant or substantial caring tasks and assume a level of responsibility, which would usually be associated with an adult. The person receiving care is often a parent, but can be a sibling, grandparent or other relative who is disabled, has some chronic illness, mental health problem or other condition connected with a need for care, support or supervision' (Becker, 2000, p 378).

[8] This was particularly the case in lone-parent families, where the lone parent was ill or had a disability, or in families who had little or no access to any other sources of informal care or support (see Becker et al, 1998).

[9] Indeed, up until the second half of the 20th century, research into the impacts of parental illness or disability on children had been conducted mainly from within the field of clinical and psychological research, and relied in the main on laboratory work or observations (see Anthony, 1970; Sturges, 1978).

[10] The research would be located at the inclusive ('participant as actor', PAA) domain, and intersecting between this and the recognition ('participant as subject', PAS) domains, as outlined in the Participatory Model in Chapter Six, Figure 6.1.

[11] Evidence from the first study, *Children who care: Inside the world of young carers* (Aldridge and Becker, 1993), led to an Early Day Motion in Parliament calling on the government to recognise and support informal child carers.

[12] Members of the Young Carers Research Group have provided evidence on young caring to the Standing Commission on Carers Preliminary Pre-legislative Scrutiny Committee (2013). This has resulted in the needs of young carers being included in both the Care and Support Bill and the Children and Families Bill.

[13] For example, on 24 January 2013, a panel of young adult carers was invited to recount their experiences of caring and to present their views at a national seminar on young adult caring chaired by HRH the Princess Royal (and jointly hosted by the National Institute of Adult Continuing Education [NIACE] and the Carers Trust).

[14] Thus ensuring participants' anonymity and confidentiality, gaining informed consent, ensuring the safe storage of data (under the Data Protection Act 1998), in accordance with Rethink guidelines and Loughborough University Ethics Committee. Information to children and young people, as well as to parents and professionals, included information about the project, the right to withdraw and disclosure procedures. (Rethink was the research partner on the study.)

[15] Most recently, this has culminated in the introduction of international guidelines for researchers working with children and young people (ERIC guidelines; see Graham et al, 2013). While such guidance is both necessary and important from the perspective of researchers who are working with vulnerable children and young people, it is disappointing to see that the ERIC guidelines do not appear to have been drawn up in consultation with children and young people themselves, thus compromising the participation agenda. The consultation process involved in producing the ERIC guidelines was extensive – involving 400 researchers and other stakeholders from across the world and an expert advisory panel – but children and young people don't appear to have been among these stakeholders or 'experts' who were consulted. This underlines the point that has been made throughout this chapter, that children's contributions and rights need to be recognised in all areas of their lives, including their right to participation, and this should include their right to take part in ethical debates and practices that have direct consequences for them.

Chapter Three

[1] The term 'learning difficulty' (or 'learning difficulties') is used throughout this chapter to reflect preferences in terminology as stated by people with learning difficulties themselves. Self-advocacy studies have revealed that some people with learning difficulties do not identify with disability and its association with physical impairment (see Chappell et al, 2001). However, some researchers and commentators continue to use 'learning disability' and particularly those working in health or health care (whereas 'learning difficulty' tends to be used in education research or studies).

[2] In the context of new initiatives in health and social care, for example, Gilbert (2004, p 298) notes the significance of the introduction of the National Health Service (NHS) and Community Care Act 1990, the NHS Plan, the *Research governance framework for health and social care* and central government-promoted organisations such as INVOLVE and Folk. Us, in 'giving impetus for a number of initiatives aimed at promoting the inclusion of people with learning disabilities in research and evaluation.'

[3] The STH project was a two-year study of the therapeutic properties of horticulture conducted at various gardening projects across the UK supported by the national horticulture charity, Thrive (also the research partners on the study). These gardening projects provided horticulture therapy for a range of vulnerable groups, including people with physical disabilities, learning difficulties, mental health problems and who also experienced social exclusion. The project was funded by the Big Lottery Fund.

[4] Notably, in the photographic participation STH project, the method did not require participants to contribute verbally by 'explaining' their photographs if they did not want to or weren't able to do so. The photographic data participants produced were presented in a number of different ways, including with accompanying written narratives and as stand-alone images attributed to the participant-photographers (see Sempik et al, 2005; Aldridge, 2007). In this way, the approach would be located at the 'inclusive' level in the participatory framework or at the intersection between the inclusive and 'emancipatory' modes (see Chapter Six, Figure 6.1).

[5] Establishing and maintaining relationships with staff were equally important in the research process, not least because they worked closely with participants. Gaining access to participants was not problematic in

terms of staff intervening or 'gatekeeping' – deciding themselves whether participants could be interviewed or involved in the research based on judgements about 'best interests'. In part this was due to the nature of the project environment – often outdoor, communal spaces – and thus meeting with and talking to staff and clients alike took place in a very informal and relaxed setting, and project staff were happy for the research team to participate in activities, to talk to clients and to spend time with them.

[6] It transpired that none of the participants took photographs of themselves and very few featured other clients at the STH projects. Most photographs of other people at the projects were of project staff (consent had been obtained from these staff to include these images in outputs from the study). For a full discussion of the content and thematic analyses of the photographic data see Sempik et al (2005).

Chapter Four

[1] Domestic violence is defined here as 'Any incident or pattern of incidents of controlling, coercive or threatening behaviour, violence or abuse between those aged 16 or over who are or have been intimate partners or family members regardless of gender or sexuality. This can encompass but is not limited to the following types of abuse: psychological, physical, sexual, financial, emotional. Controlling behaviour is: a range of acts designed to make a person subordinate and/or dependent by isolating them from sources of support, exploiting their resources and capacities for personal gain, depriving them of the means needed for independence, resistance and escape and regulating their everyday behaviour. Coercive behaviour is: an act or a pattern of acts of assault, threats, humiliation and intimidation or other abuse that is used to harm, punish, or frighten their victim' (Home Office, 2012).

[2] It is important to note that both in this chapter and throughout the book I identify and refer to women victims *and* survivors of domestic violence in order to avoid subscription to a purely victimised ethic. This is also in recognition (from what we know from research and practice and from women's activism, campaigning, and so on) of the transformations that women can and do make in respect of surviving and recovering from their violent experiences. Survival has been a key aspect of feminist research and practice relating to domestic violence, which aims to locate women's experiences not just psychologically, as victimised individuals, but also socially, culturally, politically and so on, in order to emphasise that with the right kinds of support and interventions, women can and do survive

domestic violence. The intention here, then, is also to show that the barriers to women's survival are often practical and systemic, rather than simply personal, psychological or emotional.

3   It is important to emphasise that while it is now common practice to refer to women as *victims-survivors* of domestic violence, not all of the women who contributed to and took part in the PNR study (as well as the women who were involved in the mental health study on which the secondary analysis was conducted) considered themselves survivors, either because the violence was ongoing, or because they continued to experience the psychological effects of the violence once the relationship with their partner had ended, thus prolonging their sense of victimisation.

4   In methods terms, intensive qualitative approaches such as autobiographical or life story techniques provide ways of illuminating lived experience through highly personalised and subjective narrative explication. They provide in-depth insights as opposed to the breadth of data offered in extensive or, what are described as 'nomotheic', approaches (Franz and Robey, 1984, p 1214).

5   Five women have written or are currently working on their written narratives, and all completed narratives will be published in an anthology of the women's collective stories (Write It, 2015).

6   Although interpretation by the reader is inevitable when presenting written accounts (in full), and while the women's narratives have not been (and will not be) edited in the anthology, aspects of the narratives will be and have been considered and discussed in other publications as part of a multi-dimensional approach (see the full discussion in Chapter Five).

7   A tension here, however, was that the women chose not to reveal their true identities by using their own names as authors of the narratives. Thus, the emancipatory element of the study was compromised to some extent by the continuing need for anonymity, even for those women who had escaped or survived abusive relationships. For many women victims-survivors of domestic violence, even when the abusive relationship is over, this does not prevent them worrying about the consequences of disclosure even years later.

8   This approach is similar to that of Lieblich and colleagues' (1998) strategy of presenting in-full narrative accounts of research participants so that readers could compare the authors' interpretations against the narratives, and also

perform their own (reader) analyses. Here, however, the intention is to prioritise authorial (participant) 'voice' through presentation of Rosie's narrative *and* her reflections on this (see Chapter Five).

[9]   A pseudonym has been used, in accordance with the narrator's wishes.

References

Abdul-Quader, A.S., Heckathorn, D.D., Sabin, K. and Saidel, T. (2006) 'Implementation and analysis of respondent-driven sampling: lessons learned from the field', *Journal of Urban Health: Bulletin of the New York Academy of Medicine*, vol 83, no 7, pp 12-15.

Alanen, L. and Mayall, B. (eds) (2001) *Conceptualising child–adult relationships*, London: Routledge.

Alderson, P. (1995) *Listening to children: Children, ethics and social research*, Barkingside: Barnardo's.

Aldridge, J. (2006) 'The experiences of children living with and caring for parents with mental illness', *Child Abuse Review*, vol 15, no 2, pp 79-88.

Aldridge, J. (2007) 'Picture this: the use of participatory photographic research methods with people with learning disabilities', *Disability & Society*, vol 22, no 1, pp 1-17.

Aldridge, J. (2010) 'Consulting with young carers and their families', in S.R. Redsell, and A. Hastings (eds) *Skills for consulting with children*, London: Radcliffe Medical Press, pp 87-99.

Aldridge, J. (2012a) 'The participation of vulnerable children in photographic research', *Visual Studies*, vol 27, no 1, pp 48-58.

Aldridge, J. (2012b) 'Working with vulnerable groups in social research: dilemmas by default and design', *Qualitative Research*, pp 1-19.

Aldridge, J. (2013) 'Identifying the barriers to women's agency in domestic violence: the tensions between women's personal experiences and systemic responses', *Social Inclusion*, vol 1, no 1, pp 3-12.

Aldridge, J. (forthcoming, 2015) *Write It: An anthology of women's writing on surviving domestic violence*, Loughborough: Loughborough University.

Aldridge, J. and Becker, S. (1993) *Children who care: Inside the world of young carers*, Loughborough: Young Carers Research Group, Loughborough University.

Aldridge, J. and Becker, S. (1994) *My child, my carer*, Loughborough: Young Carers Research Group, Loughborough University.

Aldridge, J. and Becker, S. (2003) *Children who care for parents with mental illness: Perspectives of young carers, parents and professionals*, Bristol: Policy Press.

Aldridge, J. and Cross, S. (2008) 'Young people today: media, policy and youth justice', *Journal of Children and Media*, vol 2, no 3, pp 203-18.

Aldridge, J. and Dearden, C. (2013) 'Disrupted childhoods', in M. Pickering and E. Keightley (eds) *Memory research in cultural studies*, Edinburgh: Edinburgh University Press, pp 167-84.

Aldridge, J. and Sharpe, D. (2007) *Pictures of young caring*, Loughborough: Young Carers Research Group, Loughborough University.

Aldridge, J. and Wates, M. (2004) 'Young carers and their disabled parents: moving the debate on', in T. Newman and M. Wates (eds) *Disabled parents and their children: Building a better future*, Ilford: Barnardo's.

Allen, M. (2011) *Narrative therapy for women experiencing domestic violence: Supporting women's transitions from abuse to safety*, London: Jessica Kingsley Publishers.

Anthony, E.J. (1970) 'The impact of mental and physical illness on family life', *American Journal of Psychiatry*, vol 127, no 2, pp 138-46.

APA (American Psychiatric Association) (2001) *Diagnostic and statistical manual of mental disorders* (4th edn, revised) (DSM-IV-T), Washington, DC: APA.

Arnot, M. and Reay, D. (2007) 'A sociology of pedagogic voice: power, inequality and pupil consultation', *Discourse: Studies in the Cultural Politics of Education*, vol 28, no 3, pp 311-25.

Aspis, S. (2000) 'Researching our own history: who is in charge?', in L. Brigham (ed) *Crossing boundaries: Change and continuity in the history of learning disabilities*, Kidderminster: BILD Publications, pp 1-6.

Atkinson, D. (1986) 'Engaging competent others: a study of the support networks of people with a mental handicap', *British Journal of Social Work*, vol 16, supplement, pp 83-101.

Atkinson, D. (1997) *An auto/biographical approach to learning disability research*, Aldershot: Ashgate.

Atkinson, D. and Williams, F. (1990) *Know me as I am: An anthology of prose, poetry and art by people with learning difficulties*, Sevenoaks: Hodder & Stoughton.

Baldwin, C. (2013) *Narrative social work: Theory and application*, Bristol: Policy Press.

Bancroft, L. (2002) *'Why does he do that?' Inside the minds of angry and controlling men*, New York: The Berkley Publishing Group.

Banks, M. (2001) *Visual methods in social research*, London: Sage.

Banks, M. (1995) *Visual research methods*, Guildford: University of Surrey (Sru.soc.surrey.ac.uk/SRU11/SRU11.html).

Banyard, K. (2010) *The equality illusion: The truth about women and men today*, London: Faber & Faber.

Barry, M. (2001) *Young people's views and experiences of growing up*, York: Joseph Rowntree Foundation (www.jrf.org.uk/publications/young-peoples-views-and-experiences-growing).

Barton, D. and Papen, U. (2010) *The anthropology of writing: Understanding textually-mediated worlds*, London: Continuum.

Becker, S. (2000) 'Young carers', in M. Davies (ed) *The Blackwell encyclopaedia of social work*, Oxford: Blackwell, p 378.

Becker, S., Aldridge, J. and Dearden, C. (1998) *Young carers and their families*, Oxford: Blackwell Science.

Benbasat, I., Goldstein, D.K. and Mead, M. (1987) 'The case research strategy in studies of information systems', *MIS Quarterly*, vol 11, no 3, pp 369-86.

Biggs, S. (1989) *Resource-poor farmer participation in research: A synthesis of experiences from nine national agricultural research systems*, OFCOR (On-Farm Client-Oriented Research) Comparative Study Paper 3, The Hague: International Service for National Agricultural Research.

Bilsborrow, S. (1992) *'You grow up fast as well...' Young carers on Merseyside*, Liverpool: Carers National Association, Personal Services Society and Barnardo's.

Birren, J.E. and Birren, B.A. (1996) 'Autobiography: exploring the self and encouraging development', in J. Birren, G. Kenyon, J.E. Ruth, J. Schroots and T. Svensson (eds) *Aging and biography*, New York: Springer, pp 283-300.

Boddy, J. and Oliver, C. (2010) *Research governance in children's services: The scope for new advice*, London: Thomas Coram Research Unit, Department for Education (www.gov.uk/government/uploads/system/uploads/attachment_data/file/182165/DFE-RR072.pdf).

Boddy, J., and Smith, M. (2008) 'Asking the experts: developing and validating parental diaries to assess children's minor injuries', *International Journal of Social Research Methodology*, vol 11, no 1, pp 63–77.

Bolton, G. (1999) *The therapeutic potential of creative writing: Writing myself*, London: Jessica Kingsley Publishers.

Bolton, G. (2006) 'Narrative writing: reflective enquiry into professional practice', *Educational Action Research*, vol 14, no 2, pp 203-18.

Bolton, G. (2010) *Reflective practice: Writing and professional development* (3rd edn), London: Sage.

Bolton, G., Field, V. and Thompson, K. (eds) (2006) *Writing works: A resource handbook for therapeutic writing workshops and activities*, London: Jessica Kingsley Publishers.

Bolton, G., Field, V. and Thompson, K. (eds) (2011) *Writing routes: A resource handbook of therapeutic writing*, London: Jessica Kingsley Publishers.

Booth, T. (1996) 'Sounds of still voices: issues in the use of narrative methods with people who have learning difficulties', in L. Barton (ed) *Disability and society: Emerging issues and insights*, Sociology Series, New York: Longman, pp 237-55.

Booth, T. and Booth, W. (2003) 'In the frame: PhotoVoice and mothers with learning disabilities', *Disability & Society*, vol 18, no 4, pp 431-42.

Bourdieu, P. (1996) 'Understanding', *Theory, Culture & Society*, vol 13, no 2, pp 17-37.

Bragg, S. and Buckingham, D. (2008) '"Scrapbooks" as a resource in media research with young people', in P. Thomson (ed) *Doing visual research with children and young people*, Abingdon: Routledge, pp 114-31.

Britzman, D. (1989) 'Who has the floor? Curriculum teaching and the English student teacher's struggle for voice', *Curriculum Inquiry*, vol 19, no 2, pp 143-62.

Brown, S. (1998) *Understanding youth and crime*, Buckingham: Open University Press.

Burgos-Debray, E. (1984) *I, Rigoberta Menchú: An Indian woman in Guatemala* (translation by Ann Wright), London: Verso.

Campbell, R. and O'Neill, M. (2006) *Sex work now*, London: Willan Publishing.

Campbell, R. and Wasco, S.M. (2000) 'Feminist approaches to social science: epistemological and methodological tenets', *American Journal of Community Psychology*, vol 28, no 6, pp 773-51.

Catalani, C. and Minkler, M. (2010) *Photovoice: A review of the literature*, London: Centre for Narrative Research, University of East London (www.uel.ac.uk/cnr).

Centre for Narrative Research (2011) (www.uel.ac.uk/cnr/index.htm).

Chappell, A.L. (2000) 'The emergence of participatory methodology in learning disability research: understanding the context', *British Journal of Learning Disabilities*, vol 28, no 1, pp 38-43.

Chappell, A.L., Goodley, D. and Lawthom, R. (2001) 'Making connections: the relevance of the social model of disability for people with learning difficulties', *British Journal of Learning Disabilities*, vol 29, no 4, pp 45-50.

Chataway, C. (1997) 'An examination of the constraints on mutual inquiry in a participatory action research project', *Journal of Social Issues*, vol 53, no 4, pp 747-65.

Chevalier, J.M. and Buckles, D.J. (2013) *Participatory action research: Theory and methods for engaged enquiry*, Abingdon: Routledge.

Christensen, P. and Prout, A. (2002) 'Working with ethical symmetry in social research with children', *Childhood*, vol 9, no 4, pp 477-97.

Clark, A. (2011) 'Multimodal map making with young children: exploring ethnographic and participatory methods', *Qualitative Research*, vol 11, no 3, pp 311-30.

Clark, A. and Moss, P. (2001) *Listening to children: The Mosaic approach*, London: National Children's Bureau.

Clark, A. and Moss, P (2005) *Spaces to play: More listening to young children using the Mosaic approach*, London: National Children's Bureau.

Collier, J. and Collier, M. (1986) *Visual anthropology: photography as a research method,* Albuquerque: University of New Mexico Press.

Cornwall, A. and Jewkes, R. (1995) 'What is participatory research?', *Social Science & Medicine*, vol 41, no 12, pp 1667-76.

Convention on The Rights of Disabled People (2008) http://www.un.org/disabilities/convention/conventionfull.shtml

Corsaro, W.A. and Molinari, L. (2008) 'Entering and observing in children's worlds: a reflection on a longitudinal ethnography of early education in Italy', in P. Christensen and A. James (eds) *Research with children: Perspectives and practices* (2nd edn), London: Routledge, pp 239-59.

Cotterill, P. and Letherby, G. (1993) 'Weaving stories: personal auto/biographies in feminist research', *Sociology*, vol 27, no 1, pp 67-79.

CPAG (Child Poverty Action Group) (2013) *Child poverty facts and figures*, London: CPAG (www.cpag.org.uk/child-poverty-facts-and-figures).

CRC (Children's Research Centre, Open University) (2013) Research by Children & Young People (www.open.ac.uk/researchprojects/childrens-research-centre/research-children-young-people).

Crosby, R.A., Salazar, L.F., DiClemente, R.J. and Lang, D.L. (2010) 'Balancing rigor against the inherent limitations of investigating hard-to-reach populations', *Health Education Research*, vol 25, no 1, pp 1-5.

Dearden, C. and Becker, S. (1995) *Young carers: The facts*, Sutton: Reed Business Publishing.

Dearden, C. and Becker, S. (1998) *Young carers in the UK: A profile*, London: Carers National Association.

DfE (Department for Education) (2003) *Every child matters*, London: The Stationery Office (www.education.gov.uk/consultations/downloadableDocs/EveryChildMatters.pdf).

DH (Department of Health) (2000) *No secrets: Guidance on developing and implementing multi-agency policies and procedures to protect vulnerable adults from abuse*, London: DH.

DH (2004) *Research governance framework for health and social care. Implementation plan for social care*, London: DH (www.dh.gov.uk/ prod_consum_dh/groups/dh_digitalassets/@dh/@en/documents/ digitalass et/dh_4109577.pdf).

DH (2005) *Research governance framework for health and social care*, London: DH (www.dh.gov.uk/prod_consum_dh/groups/dh_digitalassets/@ dh/@en/documents/digitalasset/dh_4122427.pdf).

Dobash, R.E. and Dobash, R.P. (1992) 'Women, violence and social change', in J. Orford (ed) *Treating the disorder, treating the family*, Baltimore, MD: The Johns Hopkins University Press, pp 169-93.

Dodd, T., Nicholas, S., Povey, P. and Walker A. (2004) *Crime in England and Wales 2003/2004*, London: Home Office (www.homeoffice.gov. uk/rds/pdfs04/hosb1004.pdf).

Donaldson, P.J. (2001) *Using photographs to strengthen family planning research* (https://www.guttmacher.org/pubs/journals/3317601.pdf).

Dumbleton, P. (1998) 'Words and numbers', *British Journal of Learning Disabilities*, vol 26, no 4, pp 151-3.

Durkheim, E. (1961) *Moral education: A study in the theory and application of the sociology of education* (Translated by E. Wilson and H. Schnurer), New York: The Free Press.

Dwyer, K. (1982) *Moroccan dialogues: Anthropology in question*, Baltimore, MD: The Johns Hopkins University Press.

Ellis, C. and Bochner, A.P (1992) 'Telling and performing personal stories: the constraints of choice in abortion', in C. Ellis and M.G. Flaherty, *Investigating subjectivity: Research on lived experience*, London: Sage, pp 79-89.

Ellsberg, M. and Heise, L. (2005) *Researching violence against women: A practical guide for researchers and activists*, Geneva: WHO (World Health Organization).

Emerson, E. and Robertson, J. (2011) *The estimated prevalence of visual impairment among people with learning disabilities in the UK*, London: Learning Disabilities Observatory, Department of Health (www.rnib. org.uk/aboutus/Research/reports/2011/Learn_dis_small_res.pdf).

Erikson, E.H. (1963) *Childhood and society* (2nd edn), New York: Norton.

ESRC (Economic and Social Research Council) (2010) *Framework for research ethics* [updated September 2012] (www.esrc.ac.uk/_images/ framework-for-research-ethics-09-12_tcm8-4586.pdf).

Etherington, K. (2000) *Narrative approaches to working with adult male survivors of child sexual abuse: The client's, the counsellor's and the researcher's story*, London: Jessica Kingsley Publishers.

Ezzy, D. (1998) 'Lived experience and interpretation in narrative theory: experiences of living with HIV/AIDS', *Qualitative Sociology*, vol 21, no 2, pp 169-79.

Falkov, A. (2013) *The family model handbook: An integrated approach to supporting mentally ill parents and their children*, London: Pavilion.

Fals Borda, O. (1988) *Knowledge and people's power: Lessons with peasants in Nicaragua, Mexico and Colombia*, New York: New Horizons Press.

Fine, G. A. (1995) 'Public narration and group culture: Discerning discourse in social movements', in H. Johnston and B. Klandermans (eds), *Social movements and culture*, Minneapolis, MN: University of Minnesota Press, pp. 127–143.

Finlay, L. (2002) 'Negotiating the swamp – the opportunity and challenge of reflexivity in research practice', *Qualitative Research*, vol 2, no 2, pp 209-30.

Flynn, M. (1989) *Independent living for adults with mental handicap: A place of my own*, London: Cassell.

Ford-Gilboe, M., Campbell, J. and Berman, H. (1995) 'Stories and numbers: coexistence without compromise', *Advances in Nursing Science*, vol 18, no 1, pp 14-26.

Franklin, B. (ed) (2002) *The new handbook of children's rights: Comparative policy and practice*, London: Routledge.

Franz, C.R. and Robey, D. (1984) 'An investigation of user led system design', *Communications of the ACM*, vol 27, no 12, pp 1202-17.

Fraser, H. (2004) 'Doing narrative research: analysing personal stories line by line', *Qualitative Social Work*, vol 3, no 2, pp 179-201.

Freire, P. (1970) *Pedagogy of the oppressed*, New York: Seabury Press.

French, S. (1993) 'Disability, impairment or something in between?', in J. Swain, V. Finkelstein, S. French and M. Oliver (eds) *Disabling barriers – enabling environments*, London: Sage, pp 69-77.

Gilbert, T. (2004) 'Involving people with learning disabilities in research: issues and possibilities', *Health and Social Care in the Community*, vol 12, no 4, pp 298-308.

Gile, K.J. and Handcock, M.S. (2010) 'Respondent-driven sampling: an assessment of current methodology', *Sociological Methodology*, vol 40, no 1, pp 285-327.

Gondolf, E.W. (1988) *Battered women as survivors: An alternative to treating learned helplessness*, Lanham, MD: Lexington Books.

Goodley, D. (1996) 'Tales of hidden lives: a critical examination of life history research with people who have learning difficulties', *Disability & Society*, vol 11, no 3, pp 333-48.

Goodley D. (2000) *Self-advocacy in the lives of people with learning difficulties: the politics of resilience,* Buckingham: Open University Press.

Goodley, D. (2013) 'Dis/entangling critical disability studies', *Disability & Society*, vol 28, no 5, pp 631-44.

Goodley, D. and Moore, M. (2000) 'Doing disability research: activist lives and the academy', *Disability & Society*, vol 15, no 6, pp 861-82.

Goodson, I.F. (2013) *Developing narrative theory: Life histories and personal representation,* Abingdon: Routledge.

Göpfert, M., Harrison, P. and Mahoney, C. (1999) *Keeping the family in mind: Participative research into mental ill-health and how it affects the whole family,* Liverpool: North Merseyside Community Trust, Imagine, Barnardo's and Save the Children.

Gov.uk (2013) National Citizen Service (www.gov.uk/government/get-involved/take-part/national-citizen-service).

Graham, A., Powell, M., Taylor, N., Anderson, D. and Fitzgerald, R. (2013) *Ethical research involving children* (ERIC), Florence: Innocenti, UNICEF Office of Research.

Greek, C.E. (2005) 'Visual criminology: using photography as an ethnographic research method in criminal justice settings', *Journal of Visual Culture*, vol 3, no 3, pp 213-21.

Gray, R. and Sinding, C. (2002) *Standing ovation: Performing social science research about cancer,* Walnut Creek, CA: Altamira Press.

Haaken, J. (2010) *Hard knocks: Domestic violence and the psychology of storytelling,* London: Routledge.

Hammersley, M. (2010) 'Creeping ethical regulation and the strangling of research', *Sociological Research Online*, vol 15 no 4 (www.socresonline.org.uk/15/4/16.html).

Hart, R.A. (1992) *Children's participation from tokenism to citizenship,* Florence: UNICEF Innocenti Research Centre (www.freechild.org/ladder.htm).

Hart, R.A. (2008) 'Stepping back from the ladder: reflections on a model of participatory work with children', in A. Reid, B. Bruun Jensen, J. Nikel and V. Simovska, *Participation and learning*, Rotterdam, Netherlands: Springer, pp 19-31.

Harvey, L. (2011) 'Intimate reflections: private diaries in qualitative research', *Qualitative Research*, vol 11, no 6, pp 664-82.

Haw, K. (2008) '"Voice" and video: seen, heard and listened to?', in P. Thomson (ed) *Doing visual research with children and young people,* London: Routledge, pp 192-207.

Heath, S., Charles, V., Crow, G. and Wiles, R. (2004) 'Informed consent, gatekeepers and go-betweens', Paper presented to 'The ethics and social relations of research' stream, Sixth International Conference on Social Science Methodology, Amsterdam, August .

Hegarty, K.L. and Taft, A.J. (2001) 'Overcoming the barriers to disclosure and inquiry of partner abuse for women attending general practice', *Australian and New Zealand Journal of Public Health*, vol 25, no 5, pp 433-7.

Hendrick, H. (2003) *Child welfare: Historical dimensions, contemporary debate*, Bristol: Policy Press.

Herman, J.L. (1992) 'Complex PTSD: a syndrome in survivors of prolonged and repeated trauma', *Journal of Traumatic Stress*, vol 5, no 3, pp 377-91.

Hill, M. (2006) 'Children's voices on ways of having a voice: children's and young people's perspectives on methods used in research and consultation', *Childhood*, vol 13, no 1, pp 69-89.

Hill, M., Davis, J., Prout, A. and Tisdall, K. (2004) 'Moving the participation agenda forward', *Children & Society*, vol 18, no 2, pp 77-96.

HMIC (Her Majesty's Inspectorate of Constabulary) (2014) *Everyone's business: Improving the police response to domestic abuse*, London: HMIC (www.hmic.gov.uk/wp-content/uploads/2014/03/improving-the-police-response-to-domestic-abuse.pdf).

Hoff, L.A. (2001) 'Interpersonal violence', in C.E. Koop, C.E. Pearson and M.R. Schwarz (eds) *Critical issues in global health*, San Francisco, CA: Jossey-Bass, pp 260-71.

Home Office (2011) User guide to Home Office statistics, London: Home Office (http://www.homeoffice.gov.uk/publications/science-research-statistics/research-statistics/user-guide-crime-statistics?view=Binary

Home Office (2012) *New definition of domestic violence* (www.gov.uk/government/news/new-definition-of-domestic-violence).

House of Commons Education and Skills Committee (2004) *Ninth report of session 2004-2005, volume 1*, London: House of Commons.

House of Commons Select Committee (2008) *Children beneath the radar*, 6 February (http://www.publications.parliament.uk/pa/cm200708/cmselect/cmchilsch/331/8020601.htm).

Hughes, M.J. and Jones, L. (2000) *Women, domestic violence and Posttraumatic Stress Disorder (PTSD)*, San Diego, CA: Department of Health and Human Services.

Humphries, C. and Thiara, R. (2003) 'Mental health and domestic violence: "I call it symptoms of abuse"', *British Journal of Social Work*, vol 33, pp 209-26.

Hurdley, R. (2010) 'In the picture or off the wall? Ethical regulation, research habitus and unpeopled ethnography', *Qualitative Inquiry*, vol 16, no 6, pp 517-28.

International Save the Children Alliance (2008) *Forgotten casualties of war*, London: International Save the Children Alliance.

Jahoda, A., Markova, I. and Cattermole, M. (1989) 'Day services: a purpose in life?', *Mental Handicap*, vol 17, no 4, pp 136-9.

James, A. and Prout, A. (2005) *Constructing and reconstructing childhood: Contemporary issues in the sociological understanding of childhood*, London: Routledge.

James, A., Jenks, C. and Prout, A. (1998) *Theorising childhood*, London: Polity Press.

Joanou, J.P. (2009) 'The bad and the ugly: ethical concerns in participatory photographic methods with children living and working on the streets of Lima, Peru', *Visual Studies*, vol 24, no 3, pp 214-23.

Jurowski, J.M. and Paul-Ward, A. (2007) 'PhotoVoice with vulnerable populations: addressing disparities in health promotion among people with intellectual disabilities', *Health Promotion Practice*, vol 8, no 4, pp 358-65.

Kaplan, I. (2008) 'Being "seen" being "heard": engaging with students on the margins of education through participatory photography', in P. Thomson (ed) *Doing visual research with children and young people*, Abingdon: Routledge, pp 175-91.

Kaplan, L. (1997) *The story of Jane: The legendary underground feminist abortion service*, Chicago, IL: University of Chicago Press.

Kelly, L. (2011) '"Social inclusion" through sports-based interventions?', *Critical Social Policy*, vol 31, no 1, pp 126-50.

Kiernan, C. (1999) 'Participation in research by people with learning disability: origins and issues', *British Journal of Learning Disabilities*, vol 27, pp 43-7.

Kirby, P. and Bryson, S. (2002) *Measuring the magic? Evaluating young people's participation in public decision-making*, London: Carnegie Young People Initiative.

Kitzinger, J. (1994) 'The methodology of focus groups', *Sociology of Health and Illness*, vol 16, no 1, pp 103-21.

Lakin, C. (1997) 'Rethinking intelligence and creative expression', *Impact*, vol 10, no 1, pp 4-5.

Lansdown, G. (1994) 'Children's rights', in B. Mayall (ed) *Children's childhoods: Observed and experienced*, London: Falmer Press, pp 33-44.

Larkin, M. (2009) *Vulnerable groups in health and social care*, London: Sage.

Lehrner, A. and Allen, N.E. (2008) 'Social change movements and the struggle over meaning-making: a case study of domestic violence narratives', *American Journal of Community Psychology*, vol 42, no 3-4, pp 220-34.

Leitch, R. (2008) 'Creatively researching children's narratives through images and drawings', in P. Thomson (ed) *Doing visual research with children and young people*, Abingdon: Routledge, pp 37-58.

Lewis, A. and Porter, J. (2004) 'Interviewing children and young people with learning disabilities: guidelines for researchers and multi-professional practice', *British Journal of Learning Disabilities*, vol 32, no 4, pp 191-7.

Lieblich, A., Tuval-Mashiach, R. and Zilber, T. (eds) (1998) *Narrative research: Reading, analysis, and interpretation*, London: Sage.

Lister, R. (2005) 'Growing pains', *The Guardian*, 6 October (www.guardian.co.uk/politics/2005/oct/06/children.childprotection).

Lister, R. (2013) 'Speaking truth to power: sociology and social policy in action', Public Lecture, 21 February, Loughborough: Loughborough University.

Lodge, D. (2002) 'Sense and sensibility', *The Guardian*, 2 November (www.theguardian.com/books/2002/nov/02/fiction.highereducation).

McTaggart, R. (ed) (1997) *Participatory action research: International contexts and consequences*, Albany, NY: State University of New York Press.

Madge, N., Hemming, P.J., Goodman, A., Goodman, S., Kingston, S., Stenson, K. and Webster, C. (2012) 'Conducting large-scale surveys in secondary schools: the case of the Youth on Religion (YOR) Project', *Children & Society*, vol 26, no 6, pp 417-29.

Mahon, A. and Higgins, J. (1995) *'A life of our own': Young carers: An evaluation of three RHA funded projects in Merseyside*, Manchester: University of Manchester Health Services Management Unit.

Masson, J. (2004) 'The legal context', in S. Fraser, V. Lewis, S. Ding, M. Kellett and C. Robinson (eds) *Doing research with children and young people*, London: Sage, pp 43-58.

Mayall, B. (ed) (2002) *Children's childhoods: Observed and experienced*, London: Falmer Press.

Meredith, H. (1991) 'Young carers: the unacceptable face of community care', *Social Work & Social Sciences Review*, supplement to vol 3, pp 47-51.

Mishler, E.G. (1991) *Research interviewing: Context and narrative*, Cambridge, MA: Harvard University Press.

Moore, L.W. and Miller, M. (1999) 'Initiating research with doubly vulnerable populations', *Journal of Advanced Nursing*, vol 30, no 5, pp 1034-40.

Moore, R. and Muller, J. (1999) 'The discourse of "voice" and the problem of knowledge and identity in the sociology of education', *British Journal of Sociology of Education*, vol 20, no 2, pp 189-206.

Mordoch, E. and Hall, W. (2008) 'Children's perceptions of living with a parent with a mental illness: finding the rhythm and maintaining the form', *Qualitative Health Research*, vol 18, no 8, pp 1127-44.

Morrow, V. and Richards, R. (1996) 'The ethics of social research with children: an overview', *Children & Society*, vol 10, no 2, pp 90-105.

Munro, E. (2008) 'Research governance, ethics and access: a case study illustrating the new challenges facing social researchers', *International Journal of Social Research Methodology*, vol 11, no 5, pp 429-39.

Nagar, R. and Geiger, S. (2007) 'Reflexivity and positionality in feminist fieldwork revisited', in A. Tickell, E. Sheppard, J. Peck and T. Barnes (eds) *Politics and practice in economic geography*, London: Sage, pp 267-78.

NCAS (National Care Advisory Service) (2013) *Peer research: How to make a difference*, Loughborough: SOS Children's Villages, Loughborough University (http://resources.leavingcare.org/upload s/4930033912d6945c6145340f3d6056bb.pdf).

NCB (National Children's Bureau) (2004) *Guidelines for research*, London: NCB (www.ncb.org.uk/dotpdf/open%20access%20- %20 phase%201%20only/research_guidelines_200604.pdf).

Nind, M. (2008) *Conducting qualitative research with people with learning, communication and other disabilities: Methodological challenges*, London: ESRC National Centre for Research Methods Review Paper.

Noyes, A. (2008) 'Using video diaries to investigate learner trajectories: researching the "unknown unknowns"', in P. Thomson (ed) *Doing visual research with children and young people*, Abingdon: Routledge, pp 132-145

Oakley, A. (1979) *Becoming a mother*, Oxford: Robertson.

Observer, The (2008) 'The grim reality of the child carers', 13 May, p 19.

Oliver, M. (1990) *The politics of disablement*, Basingstoke: Macmillan.

Oliver, M. (1997) 'Emancipatory research: realistic goal or impossible dream?', in C. Barnes and G. Mercer (eds) *Doing disability research*, Leeds, The Disability Press, University of Leeds, pp 15-31.

Ollerton, J. and Horsfall, D. (2013) 'Rights to research: utilising the Convention on the Rights of Persons with Disabilities as an inclusive participatory action research tool', *Disability & Society*, vol 28, no 5, pp 616-30.

O'Neill, A. (1988) *Young carers: The Tameside research*, Tameside: Tameside Metropolitan Borough Council.

O'Neill, M., Giddens, S., Breatnach, P., Bagley, C., Bourne, D. and Judge T. (2002) 'Renewed methodologies for social research: ethno-mimesis as performative praxis', *The Sociological Review*, vol 50, no 1, pp 69-88.

O'Reilly, K. (2012) *Ethnographic methods* (2nd edn), London: Routledge

Page, R. (1988) *Report on the initial survey investigating the number of young carers in Sandwell secondary schools*, Sandwell: Sandwell Metropolitan Borough Council.

Park, P. (1993) 'What is participatory research? A theoretical and methodological perspective', in P. Park, M. Brydon-Miller, B. Hall and T. Jackson (eds) *Voices of change: Participatory research in the United States and Canada*, Westport, CT: Bergin & Garvey, pp 1-19.

Parrott, L., Jacobs, G. and Roberts, D. (2008) 'Stress and resilience factors in parents with mental health problems and their children', *SCIE Research Briefing*, No 23, London: Social Care Institute for Excellence.

Patai, D. (1994) (Response) 'When method becomes power', in A. Gitlen (ed) *Power and method*, New York: Routledge, pp 61-73.

Pennebaker, J.W. (2000) 'Telling stories: the health benefits of narrative', *Literature and Medicine*, vol 19, no 1, pp 3-18.

Penrod, J., Preston, D. B., Cain, R. E., and Starks, M. T. (2003) 'A discussion of chain referral as a method of sampling hard-to-reach populations', *Journal of Transcultural Nursing*, vol 14, no 2, pp 100-7.

Pillow, W. (2003) 'Confession, catharsis or cure? Rethinking the uses of reflexivity as methodological power in qualitative research', *International Journal of Qualitative Studies in Education*, vol 16, no 2, pp 175-96.

Platt, L., Wall, M., Rhodes, T., Judd, A., Hickman, M., Johnston, L.G., Renton, A., Bobrova, N. and Sarang, A. (2006) 'Methods to recruit hard-to-reach groups: comparing two chain referral sampling methods of recruiting injecting drug users across nine states in Russia and Estonia', *Journal of Urban Health: Bulletin of the New York Academy of Medicine*, vol 8, no 7, pp 139-53.

Plummer, K. (1995) *Telling sexual stories: Power, change and social worlds*, London: Routledge.

Plummer, K. (2001) *Documents of life 2: An invitation to a critical humanism*, London: Sage.

Poindexter, C.C. (2002) 'Research as poetry: a couple experiences HIV', *Qualitative Inquiry*, vol 8, no 6, pp 707-14.

Portelli, A. (1998) *Narrative and genre*, London: Routledge.

Porter, J. and Lacey, P. (2005) *Researching learning difficulties: A guide for practitioners*, London: Sage.

Pritchard, J. and Sainsbury, E. (2004) *Can you read me? Creative writing with child and adult victims of abuse*, London: Jessica Kingsley Publishers.

Pyer, M. and Campbell, J. (2013) 'The "other" participant in the room: the effect of significant adults in research with children', *Research Ethics*, vol 9, no 4, pp 153-65.

Qvortrup, J. (1985) 'Placing children in the division of labour', in P. Close and P. Collins (eds) *Family and economy in modern society*, London: Macmillan, pp 129-45.

Radley, A. and Taylor, D. (2003) 'Images of recovery: a photo elicitation study on the hospital ward', *Qualitative Health Research*, vol 13, no 1, pp 77-99.

Raine, C. (1994) *History: The home movie project: A novel in verse*, New York: Doubleday.

Rapoport, R.N. (1970) 'Three dilemmas in action research', *Human Relations*, vol 26, no 3, pp 499-513.

Rapport, F. (2008) 'The poetry of Holocaust survivor testimony: towards a new performative social science', *Forum: Qualitative Social Research*, vol 9, no 2, article 28, pp 1-16.

Reason, P. (1998) 'Three approaches to participative inquiry', in N.K. Denzin and Y.S. Lincoln (eds), *Strategies of qualitative inquiry*, London: Sage, pp 324–39.

Reason, P. (1993) 'Reflections on sacred experience and sacred science', *Journal of Management Inquiry*, vol 2, no 3, pp 273-83.

Redwood, R. (1999) 'Narrative and narrative analysis', *Journal of Clinical Nursing*, vol 8, no 6, pp 674-84.

Richardson, L. (1994) 'Writing: a method of enquiry', in N.K. Denzin and Y.S. Lincoln (eds) *Handbook of qualitative research*, London: Sage, pp 516-29.

Richardson, M. (2000) 'How we live: Participatory research with six people with learning difficulties', Journal of Advanced Nursing, vol 32, no 6, pp 1383-1395

Rodriguez, M.D., Rodriguez, J. and Davis, M. (2006) 'Recruitment of first-generation Latinos in a rural community: the essential nature of personal contact', *Family Process*, vol 45, no 1, pp 87-106.

Rogers, A.C. (1997) 'Vulnerability, health and health care', *Journal of Advanced Nursing*, vol 27, pp 65-72.

Romito, P. (2008) *A deafening silence: Hidden violence against women and children*, Bristol: Policy Press.

Seeley, J. and Plunkett, C. (2002) *Women and domestic violence: Standards for counselling practice*, St Kilda, Victoria, Australia: The Salvation Army Crisis Services (http://wesnet.org.au/wp-content/uploads/2011/11/womendomestic_violence_counselling_standards.pdf).

Sempik, J., Aldridge, J. and Becker, S. (2005) *Health, well-being and social inclusion: Therapeutic horticulture in the UK*, Bristol: Policy Press.

Sen, P. (1999) 'Enhancing women's choices in responding to domestic violence in Calcutta: a comparison of employment and education', *The European Journal of Development Research*, vol 11, no 2, pp 65-86.

Shakespeare, T. and Watson, N. (2001) 'The social model of disability: an outdated ideology?', in S.N. Barnartt and B.M. Altman (eds) *Exploring theories and expanding methodologies: Where we are and where we need to go*, London: Emerald Group Publishing Limited, pp 9-28.

Simmons, C.A., Farrar, M., Frazer, K. and Thompson, M.J. (2011) 'From the voices of women: facilitating survivor access to IPV services', *Violence Against Women*, vol 17, no 10, pp 1226-43.

Simons, H. (2009) *Case study research in practice*, London: Sage.

Skeggs, B. (2001) 'The toilet paper: femininity, class and mis-recognition', *Women's Studies International Forum*, vol 24, no 3/4, pp 295-307.

Skovdal, M., Ogutu, V., Cellestine, A. and Campbell, C. (2009) 'Young carers as social actors: coping strategies of children caring for ailing or ageing guardians in Western Kenya', *Social Science & Medicine*, vol 69, no 4, pp 587-95.

Sparkes, A.C. and Douglas, K. (2007) 'Making the case for poetic representations: an example in action', *The Sport Psychologist*, vol 21, no 2, pp 170-90.

Spradley, J. (1979) *The ethnographic interview*, New York: Holt, Rinehart & Winston.

Stalker, K. (1998) 'Some ethical and methodological issues in research with people with learning difficulties', *Disability & Society*, vol 13, no 1, pp 5-19.

Stasiulis, D. (2002) 'The active child citizen: lessons from Canadian policy and the children's movement', *Citizenship Studies*, vol 6, no 4, pp 507-38.

Steel, R. (2001) 'Involving marginalised and vulnerable groups in research: a consultation document', *Involve*, London: NHS.

Strawson, G. (2004) 'Tales of the unexpected', *The Guardian*, Saturday 10 January (www.theguardian.com/books/2004/jan/10/society.philosophy).

Sturges, J.S. (1978) 'Children's reactions to mental illness in the family', *Social Casework*, vol 59, no 9, pp 530-36.

Sustain (2013) *Case studies* (www.sustainweb.org/growinghealth/case_studies).

Swanborn, P. (2010) *Case study research: What, why and how?*, London: Sage.

Taft, A. (2003) 'Promoting women's mental health: the challenges of intimate/domestic violence against women', *Australian Domestic and Family Violence Clearing House*, Issues Paper 8, pp 1-24.

Thomas, N. and O'Kane, C. (1998) 'The ethics of participatory research with children', *Children & Society*, vol 12, no 5, pp 336-48.

Thompson, K. (2010) *Therapeutic journal writing: An introduction for professionals*, London: Jessica Kingsley Publishers.

Thomson, P. (ed) (2008) *Doing visual research with children and young people*, London: Routledge.

Townson, L., Macauley, S., Harkness, E., Chapman, R., Docherty, A., Dias, J., Eardley, M. and McNulty, N. (2004) 'We are all in the same boat: doing "people-led" research', *British Journal of Learning Disabilities*, vol 32, no 2, pp 72-6.

Tregaskis, C. (2002) 'Social model theory: the story so far', *Disability & Society*, vol 17, no 4, pp 457-70.

TUC (Trades Union Council) (2011) *Bearing the brunt, leading the response: women and the global economic crisis*, London: TUC (www.tuc.org.uk/extras/TUC_Global-women.pdf).

Ulin, P.R., Robinson, E.T. and Tolley, E.E. (2002) *Qualitative methods in public health: A field guide for applied research*, London: Jossey-Bass.

UNICEF (1989) *United Nations Convention on the Rights of the Child* (www.unicef.org/crc).

Walker, R., Schratz, B and Egg, P. (2008) 'Seeing beyond violence: visual research applied to policy and practice', in P. Thomson (ed) *Doing visual research with children and young people*, Abingdon: Routledge, pp 164-74.

Walmsley, J. and Johnson, K. (2003) *Inclusive research with people with learning disabilities: Past, present and futures*, London: Jessica Kingsley Publishers.

Websdale, N. (1995) 'Rural women abuse: the voices of Kentucky women', *Violence Against Women*, vol 1, no 4, pp 309-38.

WHO (World Health Organization) (2001) *Putting women first: Ethical and safety recommendations for research on domestic violence against women*, Geneva: WHO (www.who.int/gender/documents/violence/who_fch_gwh_01.1/en).

WHO (2005) *WHO multi-country study on women's health and domestic violence against women* (www.who.int/gender/violence/who_multicountry_study/en).

WHO/LSHTM (London School of Hygiene and Tropical Medicine) (2010) *Preventing intimate partner and sexual violence against women: Taking action and generating evidence*, Geneva: WHO.

Whyte, W.F. (1989) 'Advancing scientific knowledge through participatory action research', *Sociological Forum*, vol 4, no 3, pp 367-85.

Wilcox, P. (2006) 'Communities, care and domestic violence', *Critical Social Policy*, vol 26, no 4, pp 722-47.

Williamson, E. (2010) 'Living in the world of the domestic violence perpetrator: negotiating the unreality of coercive control', *Violence Against Women*, vol 16, no 12, pp 1412-23.

Women's Aid (2012) *Consultation response: Universal Credit and related regulations – Response from Women's Aid*, July.

World Bank, The (1993) *World development report: Investing in health*, New York: Oxford University Press.

Wyness, M. (2006) *Childhood and society: An introduction to the sociology of childhood*, Basingstoke, UK: Palgrave Macmillan.

Yin, R.K. (2004) *The case study anthology*, London: Sage.

Index

Note: Page numbers in italic type refer to tables, page numbers followed by '*n*' suffix refer to notes.